KNOCKING
ON HEAVEN'S DOOR

(A SIMPLE GUIDE TO PRAYER)

DIANE WILKIE

Published by Open Scroll
Publications

Copyright © 2014 by Diane Wilkie

Second edition published 2015 by Open Scroll Publications Ltd,
25 Mary Street, Jewellery Quarter,
Birmingham, B3 1UD.

ISBN 978-0-9930876-6-0

The names and identifying details of some individuals
mentioned in this book have been changed to protect their privacy.

A CIP catalogue record for this book is available from the
British library.

Book cover by Nigel Wilkie and Todd Engel

Typeset by Open Scroll Publications

Email: dee.wilkie7@hotmail.co.uk

Printed in Great Britain.

DEDICATION

My beloved, I need to tell you that the very deepest depths of my soul long for you. The whole of my life has brought me to the point where I realise it's all about you, and you are all that matters now! How can I find the words to tell you how much I love you and how much you mean to me? There are no words adequate enough and I am speechless! I therefore dedicate this book to you my beautiful Lord and Saviour Jesus Christ. I want to thank you for calling me for a purpose, teaching me how to pray, and how to express all that you have taught me. This book is written in your honour Lord, for your pleasure and glory. May it bless and help your people to draw close to you, and to find renewed passion to want intimacy with you. Writing this is my way of telling you that you are everything to me! You are the most exquisite treasure anyone could ever have. I look forward to spending always and the whole of eternity with you. I adore and love you with all that I have and all that I am.

Always and forever your daughter,
Diane
x x x x

ACKNOWLEDGMENTS

To Jesus: You are the love of my life and no one compares to you! You are first and last in my life! Thank you for the plan you have for me and perfected even before I was born! Thank you for sharing your prayer secrets with me. Thank you for giving me life and for giving that life purpose and meaning. I give this life back to you, and ask you to use it to make yourself known. Have your way completely through me!

To Nigel: You are an answer to prayer! Thank you for being the best husband in the world and the man for me! Thank you for lovingly supporting me to write this book. Thank you for believing in and fighting for me. Thank you for all your encouragement, friendship and wisdom, and for allowing God to use you to show me that dreams do come true!

To Mickey: You called me a writer before I had ever written anything worthwhile. Your belief in my writing ability helped inspire me to lay hold of the gift God has given me, and refuse to let go! As a result I'm on this amazing writing adventure, and reaching for the stars. Thank you.

To mum and dad: What can I say? Thank you for your love, your support, your prayer warrior attitude and example. Thank you for your unceasing prayers....they have made me who I am today. Mummy thank you for showing me a living example of all that a godly woman should be. Thank you for giving me the courage to be the woman of God I was called and born to be!

To Luke and Samuel: You are mighty men of God and my very own miraculous answers to prayer, as well as evidence and proof that prayer works! It has been an honour and privilege to prayerfully watch over you, and it has been a humbling experience to learn to pray with you!

To Jackie: We have learned about life, walked together and you have been my prayer partner forever! Your friendship, love, faithful prayers and godly counsel have kept me going when it made perfect sense to throw in the towel and give up! You are simply an inspiration, and will never know how much you helped me to embrace my journey, in spite of all the challenges! You are worth a million sisters or friends! Thank you.

To Jason: You have loved me through some of the most impossible times of my life! Your loving concern always reminds me I have a God who loves me and will never stop, even when everything else fails! Thank you.

To Jit: You have been my faithful friend! It has been amazing to have someone who loves me just for who I am, always encouraging me to just be myself! Thank you.

To Antonio: You have been a living example of just how deeply and sincerely God loves me! You have helped me see and believe that his love for me is beautiful, uncomplicated, and simply irresistible. Thank you.

To Annmarie: Your heart is so beautiful and a constant reminder that I must guard mine with all diligence! Thank you.

To Makeda: You are as beautifully childlike as we are instructed to be, in order to even enter the kingdom of God! Thank you for your example.

To every other special person in my life, you all know who you are. Thank you for the unique gift you are to me and the sheer beautiful colour you bring to my life. This book is written for warriors of God like you, and to all who hunger and thirst for what is right. I love you all!

Matthew chapter 7 verses 7-8
Keep on asking and it will be given you, keep on seeking and you will find, keep on knocking reverently and the door will be opened to you. For everyone who keeps on asking receives; and he who keeps on knocking, (the door) will be opened.

CONTENTS

AN OPENING THOUGHT

Prayer is so much more than just something you do or participate in every now and again. Prayer is a life style that brings meaning and purpose, and goes a long way towards bringing some sense to the general challenge of life itself.

Prayer is the 'life force,' that can be likened to the engine of a car. Without it although the body of the car may look pretty impressive and promise great things, in essence it is just an empty shell going nowhere fast!

As human beings we are essentially made up of three parts; we are a spirit, we have a soul and we live in a physical body. Prayer is a spiritual exercise that is effective in the world of the spirit. Although we cannot see this world with our natural eyes, it is however one of the most real things we will ever encounter.

When someone becomes a Christian, it means they have willingly vacated the driver's seat of the car and invited Jesus to drive instead! It doesn't matter how young a person may be in the faith, sooner or later they experience and develop firsthand knowledge that essentially they live and must therefore fight in the spirit world.

This world affects absolutely everything in the natural world. In other words whatever takes place in the world of the spirit has consequences in the natural world as we know it. Unfortunately many people are totally oblivious to this truth and therefore have little or no idea that the two worlds are intimately entwined. This is one example where ignorance definitely is not bliss. Sadly as a result these very same people find themselves in the thick of things and in the heat of the battle. They are often at such an unfair disadvantage helplessly wondering what to do and where to turn. They are plagued with so many questions that don't seem to have any adequate answers. How well we fight of course, depends on the knowledge we have and therefore how equipped we are, to be able to pray effectively.

Prayer amounts to getting a higher perspective, (God's perspective) on every aspect of everyday life. Prayer is having the direct telephone and extension number to the most important person you could ever hope to meet. Moving beyond that, prayer is then taking the meeting with the Almighty to the next level, and discussing the issues of everyday life with the one who is the King of wisdom. There is something awesome about talking over the nitty gritty of life with someone who actually understands and gets you. It helps that he knows where you're coming from. There is nothing worse, than pouring your heart out to someone who is staring at you with a blank or confused expression on their face! It is liberating to pray and talk to someone who knows what you're actually talking about!

Revelation Chapter 19 verse 16
And on his garment (robe) and on his thigh he has a name (title) inscribed, KING OF KINGS AND LORD OF LORDS.

God is awesome and exercises the highest authority in the whole of heaven and earth. Living a life of prayer means being in touch with the one in whom life itself originates. Being in regular contact with him means that the answers needed to the questions of life are more readily accessible. Therefore less time is wasted just going round in circles and living in an impossible maze. Prayer therefore is a mighty force that often does make the difference between life and death.

Being a perfect prayer warrior is a noble ideal, and I truly take my hat off to whoever has acquired the reputation of having reached this status. However for the vast majority of us, it is about being an ordinary person who has had a personnel encounter with an extraordinary mighty God. Such an experience leads to a revelation of who God is. Then often there is an inevitable 'falling in love' with this God who has revealed and unveiled himself, to this 'ordinary beloved person.'

Being a simple person with a heart hungry to meet and know this amazing God, is the main qualification. If you are someone willing to pray faithfully, honestly and as sincerely as possible, you will see results and cope well with life's challenges and disappointments. This is definitely an achievable goal to set as a guideline. Of course practice makes all the difference. When you meet someone for the first time, at first you may feel shy and only comfortable chitchatting about general things. However as you get to know the person better and more intimately, your conversation changes to reflect that. This applies also to prayer until eventually you find yourself praying about everything. Suddenly it becomes the most automatic and natural thing in the world for you to do. Before you know it you find yourself begin to share your heart, and talk about private personal hopes and dreams, and about the things that matter to you the most. Soon you begin to wonder how you ever lived without the miracle that is prayer.

If you are a Christian your prayer life is vital! This is the thing that affects every other part of your life. It also affects every other life that your life encounters. Prayer is so powerful that even if you have never met someone, your prayers for them could drastically change things, and make an incredible difference to their lives the way nothing else can. For this reason prayer is not power for the fainthearted. Rather it is a mighty force for those prepared to persevere in a steadfast manner, until the answers come and the results speak for themselves.

2nd Chronicles chapter 7 verse 14
If my people, who are called by my name, shall humble themselves and pray, seek, crave, and require of necessity my face and turn from their wicked ways, then will I hear from heaven, forgive their sin and heal their land.

Prayer takes place when the simplest person takes hold of their Mighty God. If they refuse to let go of him then there will be significant change in the world of the spirit. This automatically changes the atmosphere of our natural world down here on earth.

Looking at our world today there is much reason for concern, as generally speaking it seems to have gone completely mad. The news is usually quite depressing, and the politicians seem to be trying to convince themselves more than anyone else that they really are on the right track! The good news however is that if you are a child of God you were created and born for such a time as this! Your prayers are invaluable because they are helping to keep the madness at bay as the Holy Spirit puts a lid on evil. Without that there would be a lot more visible destruction in the world in which we live. On top of that, your prayers stand between a God of justice and a world that has become accustomed to breaking all the rules. As

Almighty God hears your cries he moves to intervene in the affairs of man, pouring out mercy and providing help wherever it is desperately needed.

One night quite recently I had a dream that affected me profoundly. In the dream I had just left a house where a young man lay helplessly in bed. When I looked at his feet one of them was severely disfigured. It looked broken and twisted in an unnatural way. There was no way he was going to be walking any time soon. When I saw his foot, I felt so sick that I had to leave the room. That's when I left the house. I planned to go as far away as I possibly could, trying to shake the disgusting image from my mind! Just as I got outside and started to walk away, all of sudden I had the strangest feeling. I don't know why but I found myself looking up just in time to avoid being hit by something that fell directly from the sky. I felt my heart literally jump into my mouth. Suddenly I heard the Lord speak to my heart. He explained that whenever I saw a need, (no matter what it was), if I was prepared to do something about it by praying, that he would be attentive and send whatever answer was needed. He promised to do so as speedily as the leg that nearly hit me as it fell from heaven earlier. The deal was that I had to trust him enough to take him at his word. Needless to say I woke up feeling better about a lot of things that had previously been quite a challenge. I felt a renewed commitment within myself to pray more than I had ever done before.

As we study and consider together it is my deepest wish that the following will become apparent:

A/ What prayer is
B/ what happens when we pray
C/ How to pray

I hope also that you will discover that although prayer has many aspects, it does not need to be so complex that it becomes daunting, boring, or just a question of duty. That would not do prayer any justice, or make it anything more than a pointless exercise.

I hope that prayer will become the very heartbeat of your life, as you discover the incredible adventure that it can be. I also hope you discover that there is nothing that compares to communing with the awesome Almighty God. He makes it his business to answer prayers, and therefore encourages us to pray without ceasing!

Diane Wilkie

CHAPTER ONE

WHAT IS PRAYER ANYWAY?

I have found prayer to be one of the things that has enriched my life the most. It has been an unpredictable journey very much like a treasure hunt often only with vague clues to follow. The many treasures that have been unravelled through prayer have proven time and time again, how powerful and worthwhile it actually is. You just never know what will happen as a result of your prayers!

James Chapter 5 Verse 16
The prayer of a person living right with God is something powerful to be reckoned with.

It has been my experience to date that prayer can change anything where everything else has failed. One of the reasons it is so successful is because it begins at the most important place. It begins with us! Prayer deals with us and changes us first of all. It often changes our perspective, and therefore inevitably our thoughts and feelings about things. Prayer can help us become more balanced and compassionate human beings. This is a very good and vital place to start.

There have been many times when I have wanted to be a better person, or just wanted to do things differently. However in spite of all the best intentions in the world, I have often found myself utterly powerless to achieve anything.

Learning to pray about all areas of concern has become a major key for dealing with the most challenging things! I have found this has given me hope and enabled me to take courage, instead of becoming so discouraged that I just fainted in despair and self loathing. I have had countless issues that have arisen in my dealings with other people. Many times my relationships have challenged the very core of my being, and exposed the imperfection of human nature, in them and in me. This has often not been pretty. The only solution I have found that makes any difference has been the power of prayer. Every time I have taken an issue to the Lord, he has always helped me to take an honest and objective look at myself. As he has dealt with me I have been able to see that the problem has not necessarily been everyone else, as I originally thought. Actually at times the problem has been more me than perhaps I would have liked to admit! Heartfelt prayer however has been powerful enough to bring about a definite change. It has enabled me to see myself as an imperfect human being with faults, just like everyone else. The revelation is not given by the Lord to discourage me, rather it is given to motivate me enough to want to co-operate with him to bring about the necessary changes in me! Praise God as he changes me to be more like him every day! I now know and believe that prayer changes us into his image, and our hearts towards others.

I have seen the Lord do incredible things that I thought were impossible, and it is so exciting to discover that there really is nothing that he cannot do! As well as changing me he can and often does change others. He can change any given situation or circumstance at any given time. He is not limited or bound by the limitations of humanity.

The thrill of experiencing answered prayer has spurred me on to pray more, and to put into practise all that I have learned and continue to learn. It is these things that I would like to share with you. If you can learn to pray well and effectively, and experience the joy of answered prayer, I truly believe with all my heart it will change your life forever! It is impossible to have prayerful communication with Almighty God, and there be no effect on you and your life, as well as the lives of those for whom you pray. I have witnessed and experienced my own life changed beyond all recognition, simply because of the power of prayer. I have witnessed the changed lives of countless others, as the power of prayer has taken hold of them and those they have prayed for.

1st Thessalonians Chapter 5 verse 17
Pray all the time.

We are encouraged never to stop praying, so why do we as God's people often pray so little? Perhaps it is because we often fail to realise the incredible power residing within a 'praying Christian!'

I am reminded of Moses and the problems he ran into when trying to bring the children of Israel out of Egypt. Just when they thought they had escaped from all their hardships, they looked around and saw that Pharaoh their enemy was pursuing them. They became trapped between Pharaoh behind them, and the red sea in front of them. There was no apparent way out and they had run out of options. They began to panic and speak foolishly, as we often do when we are afraid and under pressure. It could not have been easy for Moses to lead such a people anywhere. To make matters worse because of fear, the people became aggressive and turned on him. They blamed him for the situation they found themselves in. How typical of human nature! Wisely, Moses went to God for help with this new development and dilemma. He desperately needed an answer, and he knew it was not likely to come from anywhere else.

Exodus Chapter 14 Verse 15 – 16
God said to Moses : Why cry out to me? Speak to the Israelites. Order them to get moving. Hold your staff high and stretch your hand over the sea: Split the sea! The Israelites will walk through the sea on dry ground.

It appears that God did not hand Moses the answer on a silver platter, nor did he allow Moses to indulge in a 'wet fish' attitude! The answer he gave him came instead in the form of a challenging question. Moses was encouraged by God to take a step back and look at what he had available to him. In order to be able to see clearly, Moses had to focus rather than panic. This was no time to be unable to see the wood for the trees! Only then was he able to locate the (peace deep inside himself) and to calm his raging emotions! Only then was he be able to see that he did actually have God's presence and therefore God's anointing (equipping) to do the job at hand.

Moses and the Israelites were no different from you and me. For a while they seemed to completely forget what they had access to as the people of God. This led them to become distressed and afraid of what they could see from a natural point of view. How many times do we allow ourselves to become overwhelmed by 'unfavourable or inconvenient' circumstances? How many times do we allow ourselves to be overtaken by fear as we imagine the worst possible thing happening to us? I have lost count how many times I have done exactly that and then found that fear was happy to dominate me!

The Lord had to remind Moses that he had a rod in his hand, symbolic of the power at his disposal. Thankfully we have the end of the story recorded for us. We know that once Moses remembered who he was in God, and used the rod that God had given him, he was able to take charge and control of the situation. He no longer stood around helplessly being controlled by his circumstance.

As Christians we are not 'helpless' victims unable to enjoy life, or make a real difference to the people around us. We need to see prayer as a powerful 'life changing' rod in our hands that will part any Red sea before us.

2nd Chronicles chapter 7 Verse 14
If my God-defined people, respond by humbling themselves, praying, seeking my presence, and turning their backs on their wicked lives, I'll be there ready for you: I'll listen from heaven, forgive their sins, and restore their land to health.

The Lord God himself tells us that if we his people, will allow ourselves to become a people of prayer who are walking right before him, he will hear and respond to us, doing for us what we cannot do for ourselves.

We only have to turn on the television, radio, or pick up a newspaper, to see that the world in which we live in is behaving as if everything is out of control. As Christians, we need to ask ourselves whether we are we willing to rise to the challenge to pray until we see much needed changes, hope restored, and the perfect will of our God done on this earth, even as it is done in heaven.

In my experience I have found prayer to be a beautiful and rewarding experience, and one that I thoroughly recommend. The key is to keep it simple, be persistent, and allow it to be interwoven into the very fabric of your lifestyle. I guarantee you will have no regrets, because the Lord is faithful and will meet you at the point of your need, even as he promised in:

Jeremiah chapter 29 verses 12-13
When you call on me, when you come and pray to me, I'll listen. When you come looking for me, you'll find me. Yes when you get serious about finding me and want it more than anything else, I'll make sure you won't be disappointed. God's decree.

The Lord himself will equip us to become a 'spiritual force' to be reckoned with! Have you ever felt closed in by circumstances and wondered which way to turn? Have you ever felt as if a dark cloud has come over you and is trying to suck the very life, joy and peace out of you? Personally I have felt like that so many times, I have literally lost the will, motivation or energy to believe there could possibly be any light, at the end of this particular tunnel. I'm delighted to be able to say that I have however survived each ordeal. Prayer always provides the means to go forward as well as the answer to the problem! Please however don't take my word for it though, try it and see for yourself.

Matthew chapter 7 verses 7-8
Keep on asking and it will be given you, keep on seeking and you will find, keep on knocking reverently and the door will be opened to you. For everyone who keeps on asking receives, and he who keeps on seeking finds, and to him who keeps on knocking, the door will be opened.

We are encouraged to bring to God all the things that worry, bother and concern us. When we open our heart to him and share these things with him, we have the promise that we will find the answer we are looking for. We are not to allow life to beat us down as we face it all alone. Instead we are to pray, (involving God and inviting him into our situation, no matter how challenging or scary). As we do this we will surely see the difference it makes as he works it all out for us. Do you have a problem pressing you in on every side? Does this problem refuse to go away by wishful thinking? Child of God..... What is that in your hand?

CHAPTER TWO

PRAYER IS COMMUNICATING WITH GOD

James chapter 1 verse 17
Every desirable and beneficial gift comes out of heaven. The gifts are rivers of light cascading down from the father of light. There is nothing deceitful in God, nothing two faced, nothing fickle.

The most precious and crucial thing in my life is my relationship with the Lord Jesus Christ! Even though there have been times when I have lost everything else that I held dear, I have still found myself to be the richest and most blessed woman on this earth. The reason is because everything I could ever need, or hope for, I find in him. Therefore whenever it has come down to a choice between my deep love for him on the one hand, and anyone else on the other, he has always come first and won! When he said, "You shall have no other gods before me, I have chosen to take that command very seriously. However this has often caused major problems. There have been many misunderstandings with other people as a result. In spite of the inevitable challenges as well as the personal cost, still there is only one conclusion I have been able to come to. Jesus has continually proven to be worth every ache my heart has felt, each time it has broken!

Other relationships, peace, joy, love, self esteem, and self worth, my very life itself, all flow out from the vital relationship that I have with him. Jesus is my lifeline and the source of everything good and wholesome in my life. Without him I have nothing of worth, and am constantly threatened by the possibility of losing whatever I do have. Without him that fear is free to taunt, torment, drive, and dominate my life permeating everything, ruining any slight chance I have to be happy, fulfilled and complete. Just when I grasp at straws convincing myself that all is well, some brand new horror makes is presence felt. Without him, I am completely vulnerable and open to whatever wishes to attack me at that particular time.

In every relationship there must be communication to maintain it, otherwise it fizzles out and breaks down. If there are no phone calls, love letters, times of intimacy and display of affection, then what started out as a raging fire, becomes nothing more than a desperate flicker of dashed hope, of what could have been.

A relationship with the Lord is no different. It thrives on communication and needs all of the above to survive. Spending time reading the Bible, (the greatest love letter ever written from his heart to yours), calling the Lord and talking to him intimately and affectionately, will inevitably set the deepest part of you on fire! I have found that when I wanted passion, the Lord proved to be the most passionate person I know, and matched my passion effortlessly. He left me breathless, and took me to exhilarating heights I never thought were possible in this life!

There is no one on earth who satisfies the deepest part of my soul like my Jesus! No one on earth is equipped or meant to have that place in my heart that belongs to him. Unfortunately at times I did not realise this, and misunderstood the full consequences of making the mistake of not grasping this fully. Therefore the personnel cost often has been extremely expensive and left parts of my heart and soul completely shattered. Thank God for Jesus though who has always known how to put me back together again, stronger than ever and even more determined to serve him.

HOWEVER I MUST WARN YOU! When it comes to this special relationship with the Lord you get out what you put in. To put it another way, if you pay for a cheap gold plated ring you can't expect to leave the shop with an authentic ring of pure gold. The type of relationship you have with the Lord depends on what you want, and how much you are willing to invest in him.

Matthew chapter 6 verse 6
But when you, pray, go into your most private room, and closing the door, pray to your father, who is in secret, and your father who sees in secret, will reward you in the open.

We are told to shut ourselves away to ensure we spend quality time alone with the Lord, away from distractions, and everything and everyone else. However, as soon as you become serious about your relationship with the Lord and prayer, it will often seem as if all of hell has been unleashed against you! It is not just a coincidence or just your imagination. Rather it is an unfortunate reality. The last thing the Devil wants is for your relationship with the Lord to develop because this is a huge threat to him. He will therefore oppose you on every side, trying to get to you through every opportunity possible! The plus side (and there are many) is that the closer you get to the Lord, the stronger you will become because his strength will now be available to you. After spending time alone with God, you will suddenly find you now have the strength to do everything required of you. You will become strong enough to resist the devil every time he comes against you. At last you will have the strength to live the life of victory that God has planned for you! The abundant life that he promised to give you will be your experience and your reality, rather than just a question of wishful thinking!

He (The Devil) will try every distraction he can think of to throw you off track. If that fails to work he will try to deceive you into thinking that perhaps prayer just isn't for you after all! If there is one thing I am certain of it is that the Devil is a liar! Whether you have known the Lord for ten years or just over a week, I want to encourage you to hang on in there and absolutely refuse to give up. You will have to be very determined about this because it is the only way you will overcome the obstacles. Do not allow yourself to be caught unawares! Stick close to God and you will become aware of all his tricks and tactics. Ignore the doorbell, take the phone off the hook, reject and rebuke every thought that you know is not of God and in line with his word. Sometimes it is necessary to do so out loud, to be able to regain control of your mind and bring every thought back in line with the task at hand.

It is also very important for the devil to know where you stand because of what comes out of your mouth! After all he cannot read your mind. You will therefore find saying something like this very effective:

"I declare that the blood of Jesus which is filled with God's mighty power, is against every trick and all tactics of every spirit of distraction. I declare that the kingdom of God and his perfect will for my life is in operation this day, for Jesus name sake."

(More on the power of the blood of Jesus later.)

Mark chapter 1 verse 35
The next morning Jesus awoke long before day break and went out alone into the wilderness to pray.

Luke chapter 5 verse 16
But Jesus often withdrew to the wilderness for prayer.

These scriptures show the commitment Jesus had as well as the determination to rule out any distractions. When he walked this earth as a man he found it vital to spend time alone with his father. He made and took the time to do so because it equipped him to do all that was required of him. Prayer also helped him to stay in agreement with God.

Learn to speak the word of God. Get to know your bible so that you can accurately speak the promises contained in it, over your own life! You will be so surprised at the sheer power it contains and what it can and will accomplish, as it is spoken into the atmosphere. Remember it was the very thing that God used to create the world in the beginning.

I encourage you to be bold and strong in the Lord. Stand your ground knowing that you are using the authority and power of the name and blood of Jesus. Satan understands authority, and knows that Jesus is the ultimate authority. He has firsthand knowledge of this based on his defeat, and I'm sure the memory is still fresh in his mind. He knows that he will have to leave you alone, and bow his knee before the king of kings and the Lord of Lords, who is in control of your life! However he is not always very sure what you know, and whether or not you understand what you have at your disposal. He is unsure of whether you know your spiritual position and all the benefits of being 'In Christ!' This is why a major key would be to declare your rights out loud! That way Satan will know he has no choice but to back off and remove himself from your circumstances and life!

As you begin to spend time in the Lord's presence you will get to know him. Remember this is a relationship with a real person! I have yet to discover anything more awesome or beautiful than getting to know the Lord intimately for myself. I have never met anyone like him, or anyone that compares to him. No-one gives me what he does. No-one interests or excites me the way he does!

You will soon become familiar with his likes and dislikes, as well as what he thinks about you and every aspect of your life. It is during such a time that you can pour out and express your innermost feelings to him, whether it be through praise or worship. Equally it may be an opportunity to share your hurts, disappointments and troubles. Indeed if ever there was a time, this is the time to lay everything at his feet, and rest your battle worn, battered and weary soul.

During this time Jesus will show you how to maximise your potential. He will teach you how to make the most of yourself and your time, in the most fruitful and constructive way. As a result even in this challenging modern day, you will become equipped to deal with life rather than be overwhelmed by it.

The Lord will search your heart and reveal it to you, bringing you face to face with your failure, as well as your human limitations. He doesn't do this to discourage or crush you. However unless he actually shows us the truth about our own hearts we won't be aware of their true state! It is vital to be humble enough to develop a willingness to make any necessary changes. The truth is that contrary to popular belief, being ignorant actually is not bliss. It just means we find ourselves going round and round in circles instead, incapable of making any real progress, or of truly being happy or fulfilled.

Jeremiah chapter 17 verse 9 & 10
The heart is hopelessly dark and deceitful, a puzzle that no one can figure out. But I God search the heart and examine the mind. I get to the heart of the human. I get to the root of things. I treat them as they really are, not as they pretend to be.

This can be and often is a very painful process, but one that must take place if we are to move on and forward in him. We need to acknowledge and confess our sins to the Lord, even as he points them out. We do this to be able to get release from the terrible weight and burden that sin places upon us. This is the only way we can really get close to him, because he is a holy God who cannot bear the sight of sin. If we refuse to humble ourselves and allow him to help us deal with the wrong things in our lives, then these very things will separates us from him. As we continue to spend time praying, he will deal with our hearts again and again. As we give him permission and allow him to, he will change us for the better. This process eventually will enable us to draw closer and closer to the Lord our God. This fulfils one of his deepest desires, as he created us to be close to him.

Our prayer time is the time to ask the Lord for specific things as well as the time to intercede for others, (which we will cover in later chapters).

John chapter 10 verse 27
My sheep recognise my voice. I know them and they follow me.

As we spend time communicating with the Lord, we will get to know his voice and hear from him the answers to our prayers. BEWARE!!!! God will never say anything to us that contradicts his word, so we must test what we hear. Indeed there will be many voices that we will hear along our life's journey. Not all however will be authentic, because the enemy of our soul desires to distract and deceive us. The challenge of course is being able to work out which is which. The only way to get to know God's voice is to familiarise ourselves with his word. We must therefore make spending quality time reading the bible a priority. That way if any other voice, tries to deceive you, it will sound like a completely flat tune in the middle of a beautiful melody!

We will often have to work hard at keeping the line of communication open between ourselves and the Lord. It is good to get into the habit of sharing everything with him including our thought life as a rule. That way we will develop an intimacy with him that constantly reminds us of his presence. We will also learn what it means to pray without ceasing as we go about our everyday life.

It is important to remember that all we will ever need, we will find in Jesus. When he lived on this earth as a man, he spent as much time as possible praying and communicating with our heavenly father. This was the secret to the powerful life he lived which had the power to change history. Jesus knew how to bring heaven down to earth, and he left us his example to follow in Matthew chapter 6 verses 9-13. The Lord's prayer is so rich, as it covers every aspect of life, putting each in order of priority.

As we come before our heavenly father it is important to remember who he is. He is the God and Creator of the universe and as such we must come to him with great reverence, giving him the honour and respect he deserves.

As people of prayer we have a resource of power at our disposal that can make a tremendous difference to the world in which we live. As we start to experience answered prayer, we will become more confident. We can request that the Lord's perfect will be done in every encounter we have with other people. We can also ask him to intervene in every situation or circumstance we find ourselves or others in, to ensure that his divine authority is brought to bear on everything.

The Lord knows everything including what is best in each given situation. He also sees what is around the corner so it makes sense and is wise to invite him to get involved in all that concerns us. As our human knowledge and understanding is limited, it is foolish and risky to depend totally on that alone!

Any good parent ensures that their children are provided for in terms of food, clothing, warmth, a loving home, and anything else they could possibly need. Our heavenly father is the perfect parent, and longs to give to us often more than we actually are prepared to receive. It is right to go to the Lord about our every need. He is our source and is delighted to provide for us. There is nothing that is too hard for him. Personally I have found that as a good father he does not always give me everything that I want, but he most definitely meets all my needs.

When we present ourselves before the Lord, it is very important to know that we can come honestly and just as we. We must remember that he knows everything there is to know about us anyway, so there is no point trying to hide anything from him. The good news is that he loves us with a perfect love. So nothing we do will ever make him love us any more or less than he already does. Knowing and embracing this truth is liberating because I have always longed for someone with whom I could just be myself (regardless of my human imperfections)!

Therefore we need to be prepared to acknowledge our faults before him and ask him to forgive us. He is faithful and will do so. However in the same way that he forgives us for our shortcomings, he requires us to extend the same forgiveness to other people when they hurt or wrong us. We cannot hold on to grudges, or allow ourselves to become bitter towards anyone. In the same way he expresses his continuing love towards us, even when we don't deserve it, he expects us to treat other people in the same way. It makes no difference if they are the most challenging, annoying and undeserving people we come across! The same rule applies and the lord expects us to treat them just as well as he treats us! Why? Well basically someone has to break the cycle. The truth is that the most powerful spiritual weapon we have available to use is love. Love knocks the wind out of the sails of all that is evil!

Satan the enemy of our soul desires to harm, kill and destroy us. He is always thinking of new plans and schemes to do so, and it takes the love and protection of our heavenly father to keep us safe. We need the Lord to point out all the enemy's traps and tricks, so that we don't get caught out. It is not helpful to only realise the truth when it is too late! If we stick close to God he will guide us and keep us safe.

When we pray if we follow the example that Jesus gave us, then we'll find that our prayer is wholesome and covers the main areas of our lives.

One of the most beautiful things that happens when we spend time in communication with the King of kings, is that we begin to radiate his glory. In other words his beauty can be seen on us because he is the light which rubs off on us.

Numbers chapter 6 verse 24-26
The Lord bless you and watch, guard and keep you, and the Lord make his face to shine upon and enlighten you and be gracious (kind, merciful, and giving favour) to you, The Lord lift up his approving countenance upon you and give you peace (tranquillity of heart and life continually).

3rd John chapter verse 2
Beloved I pray that you may prosper in every way and that your body may keep well, even as I know your soul keeps well and prospers.

I believe that the primary advantage of being with the Lord and spending time with him, basking in his presence and soaking up his intense love for us, is that it has such an incredible effect on us. It affects us so profoundly that it can visibly be seen, so that even our physical bodies begin to reflect what is going on inside us. The truth of the scriptures are fully realised and fulfilled in us.

Exodus chapter 34 verses 29-35
When Moses came down from Mount Sinai carrying the two tablets of the testimony, he didn't know that the skin of his face glowed because he had been speaking with God. Aaron and all the Israelites saw Moses, saw his radiant face, and held back afraid to get close to him. Moses called out to them. Aaron and the leaders in the community came back and Moses talked with them. Later all the Israelites came up to him and he passed on the commands, everything that God had told him on Mount Sinai. When Moses finished speaking with them, he put a veil over his face, but when he went into the presence of God to speak with him, he removed the veil until he came out. When he came out and told the Israelites what he had been commanded they would see Moses face, its skin glowing, and then he would again put the veil on his face until he went back in to speak with God.

This scripture is a perfect example of this. Moses had spent time with God and had received a personal revelation of his glory. (He got a special introduction to God as a person as well as to him as his God). Moses then began to reflect that glory to the point that it became obvious to others, and they were scared to even come near him. One thing is absolutely guaranteed...you cannot spend time in God's awesome presence and ever remain the same. Prayer beautifies us because the God who we are spending time with, really is the personification of beauty at its best! Communicating with God Almighty as a priority, is the key to everything good and all the treasure that we hope to find in the very fabric of our lives.

CHAPTER THREE

PRAYER IS INTERCESSION FOR OTHERS
(LITERALLY STANDING IN THE GAP)

Isaiah chapter 59 Verse 16
And he saw that there was no man and wondered that there was
no intercessor (no one to intervene on behalf of truth and right)

To intercede is to mediate as a friend between persons, and to plead the cause of another. It literally entails standing in the gap between the two parties involved. In the case of intercessory prayer it means standing in the gap in the world of 'the spirit,' standing between a person and the judgement of God. Intercession therefore can be described as love literally in action.

There are times when we see that someone is in trouble but we don't know how to pray. In those times if we will submit ourselves to the Holy Spirit and allow him to, he will pray through us, on the other person's behalf. The great thing about this is that he will pray according to his perfect will, knowledge and wisdom, concerning that person. He knows them and exactly what is needed in every single situation.

As we become mature Christians we ought to grow out of being selfish in our prayers. We can no longer justify just thinking about ourselves and what we want or need. Rather we need to be moved to pray for other people. We need to pray for those who don't know God, as well as those who know him well, but are just struggling for one reason or another. We are most like our heavenly father when we pray out of a heart filled with compassion.

One of the greatest examples of intercession in the bible is that of Moses. He mastered the art and learned that intercession was a powerful position in prayer. It was dynamic enough to cause God to change his mind, original intention and the whole outcome of an otherwise very sticky situation. The position that Moses adopted in prayer, enabled him to have a certain amount of influence with God as he respectfully reasoned with him.

Exodus chapter 32 Verse 7 – 14 & Verse 31 - 32
God spoke to Moses, "Go! Get down there! Your people whom you brought up from the land of Egypt have fallen to pieces. In no time at all they've turned away from the way I commanded them; they made a molten calf and worshipped it. They've sacrificed to it and said, these are the gods, o Israel that brought you up from the land of Egypt! God said to Moses, I look at these people oh! What a stubborn, hard headed people! Let me alone now, give my anger free reign to burst into flames and incinerate them. But I'll make a great nation out of you. Moses tried to calm his God down. He said, "Why God would you lose your temper with your people? Why you brought them out of Egypt in a tremendous demonstration of power and strength. Why let the Egyptians say, he had it in for them, he brought them out so he could kill them in the mountains, wipe them right off the face of the earth. Stop your anger. Think twice about bringing evil against your people! Think of Abraham, Isaac and Israel your servants to whom you gave your word, telling them I will give you many children, as many as the stars in the sky, and I'll give this land to your children as their land forever. And God did think twice. He decided not to do the evil he had threatened against his people.

Moses took his role as Intercessor between the disobedient and stubborn people of Israel, and a very angry Almighty God seriously. He literally stood in the gap between the two parties, and was prepared to go as far as forfeiting his own life to do so. This is the true heart of an intercessor! (Ask Jesus who knows what it really means to give everything you've got, including your life, because you love someone that much!) It takes nothing less than the mighty Spirit and deep love of God, to motivate and enable a person sufficiently, to be able to go to these lengths for someone else! How many of us would be prepared to really follow Jesus, until we mirror and reflect his sacrifice for love's sake?

Job chapter 22 verses 25-28,30
God Almighty will be your treasure, more wealth than you can imagine. You'll take delight in God, the Mighty One, and look to him joyfully, boldly. You'll pray to him and he'll listen, he'll help you do what you've promised. You'll decide what you want and it will happen; your life will be bathed in light. Yes, even the guilty will escape, escape through God's grace in your life.

Our aim needs to become getting to the place in our lives, where the Lord is the most important person in the whole world to us. He needs to be the most precious treasure that we have lives. It is then that our prayers are at their most powerful and effective. When the distinct light of his favour is shining on us, then he will answer our prayers concerning those for whom we pray, simply because of what we share with him.

Hebrews 7 Verse 23-25

Earlier there were a lot of priests, for they died and had to be replaced. But Jesus' priesthood is permanent. He's there from now to eternity to save everyone who comes to God through him, always on the job to speak up for them.

Of course Jesus is the greatest intercessor who ever lived. His prayers were one thing, but his very life of obedience was the highest prayer that could ever have been offered. It gives me deep consolation and comfort, to know that no matter what I face, Jesus takes his job to intercede for me and on my behalf very seriously!

CHAPTER FOUR

PRAYER IS MINISTERING TO THE LORD

Proverbs 15 Verse 8
The sacrifice of the wicked is an abomination, hateful and exceedingly offensive to the Lord, but the prayer of the upright is his delight!

When we love someone it is the most natural thing in the world to want to do something special for them. We often wish to show how much we appreciate having them in our lives, and to express that love to them. Sometimes words are not enough and fail to describe what we really feel for them. So we add actions to our words in an attempt to prove how important they are to us.

Our prayer time is the perfect opportunity to enjoy intimacy with the Lord. It is the best time to show him we are holding nothing back from him. During this period of communicating with him, we should aim only to minister to and bless him. We need to tell him how special, unique, beautiful, and wonderful he is. This is the time to let him know that he is the treasure that makes us rich! Jesus as mighty as he is, has feelings and can be moved and touched! Therefore he loves it when we come to him, just because we want to be with him! As awesome and powerful as he is he subjects himself to love. He doesn't approach us with walls and barriers to hide behind. He allows himself to be vulnerable to the ones he loves.

Too many times we go to him asking him for this, that and the other. We treat him as if he is a vending machine to be poked and prodded until he gives in to the whims of the spoilt brat we can all be sometimes! We should want to be near him not just because we want something, but because at that particular time there is nowhere else on earth we would rather be. The Lord loves when we come to him just because of who he is to us, and because we love him more than anything else on earth!

How many times do we actually go to him just to find out what he wants in any given situation? Do we care enough to find out what pleases him, makes him happy, and satisfies him? Do we go to him chatting our heads off, without ever taking the time to listen to him? Do we give him the chance to talk back to us? Do we even care about what is on his heart? Remember a relationship is a two way thing! No-one likes to be taken for granted or to feel used. Why should the Lord be any different? The bible warns us not to grieve the Holy Spirit of God! It wouldn't do that if hurting him wasn't possible! Perhaps it would be a good idea to periodically assess where we are at with the Lord. How much of a priority is he? Has it suddenly become all about the loaves and fish he is capable of providing?

There are many ways to minister to the Lord and we will explore some of them at this time.

Matthew Chapter 26 Verse 6 – 13
When Jesus was at Bethany, a guest of Simon the leper, a woman came up to him as he was eating dinner and anointed him with a bottle of very expensive perfume. When the disciples saw what was happening , they were furious. "That's criminal!" This could have been sold for a lot and the money handed out to the poor. When Jesus realised what was going on, he intervened. "Why are you giving this woman a hard time? She has just done something wonderfully significant for me.

You will have the poor with you every day for the rest of your lives, but not me. When she poured this perfume on my body, what she really did was anoint me for burial. You can be sure that wherever in the world the message is preached what she has just done is going to be remembered and admired.

This woman left us a perfect example to follow. The most striking thing about her was her tangible love for Jesus. This love was so real and strong that it enabled her to know exactly what would minister to him the most. Without hesitation she did just that. In spite of all the odds that were against her, the challenges, the criticism, the stares and whispers, the harsh judgement, she made her way to where she knew Jesus would be. She must have felt intimidated and misunderstood, but she remained focused because she had one thing alone on her mind. She wanted to do something meaningful and special for him. She didn't come to ask him for anything for herself or for anyone else. Her only intention was to give to him and to leave him feeling seriously blessed. Somehow she knew he needed her unique ministry and she was not about to deny him that, no matter what it cost her. What an amazing woman! The Lord's response to what she had done was, "She has done something wonderfully significant for me."

As we consider this lady let us search our own hearts and ask ourselves this question ....How often do we go to our heavenly father with the sole intention of being a blessing to him?

Psalm chapter 103 Verse 1:
Bless (affectionately, gratefully praise) the Lord, o my soul; and all that is deepest within me, bless his holy name!

In this psalm David encourages us to allow every part of us to be caught up in the wonder of our great God. It reminds us that it is possible to bless and minister to the Lord. This does not change the fact that the Lord is all sufficient and totally complete in himself. However as we are in a love relationship with him, the Lord thoroughly enjoys us. He likes when we seek him out because we enjoy his company.

HOW DO WE MINISTER TO THE LORD?

SECTION ONE:

THROUGH OUR PRAISE AND THANKSGIVING:

THANKSGIVING: Involves expressing our gratitude to God for favours and mercies.

TO PRAISE: Involves commending someone, offering a tribute of gratitude, as at the time when we worship God.

Ephesians chapter 5 Verse 20
At all times and for everything giving thanks in the name of our Lord Jesus Christ to God the Father.

If someone does something nice for us or they are good to us it is polite and good manners to say thank you. However being thankful to the Lord and generally having a thankful attitude is not something the Lord prescribes for his benefit, but it is actually for our good. Have you ever noticed how hard it is to be depressed, worried, and fearful if you are just bubbling over with gratitude? It is far easier for a thankful heart to be happy, regardless of the circumstances. An ungrateful heart is more likely to complain, focus on the negative, and be dissatisfied with everything majority of the time.

Philippians Chapter 4 Verse 6
Do not fret or have any anxiety about anything, but in every circumstance and in everything, by prayer and petition (definite

requests), with thanksgiving, continue to make your wants known to God.

It is very important to take time to reflect and thank God for all he has done for us. When we take the time to really think about it, we will often be amazed how far he has actually brought us and where he has brought us from. It is not difficult for gratitude to begin to flow freely when we think about where we would be without him. Remember in most relationships, no-one likes to be taken for granted. If we are made to feel special, it cost nothing to say thank you and express how we appreciate the person who has made us feel that way.

Psalm 111 verses 1 – 10
Hallelujah! I give thanks to God with everything I've got-
Wherever good people gather, and in the congregation. God's works are so great, worth a lifetime of study- endless enjoyment! Splendour and beauty mark his craft; His generosity never gives out. His miracles are his memorial. This God of grace, this God of love. He gave food to those who fear him, he remembered to keep his ancient promise. He proved to his people that he could do what he said: hand them the nations on a platter-a gift! He manufactures truth and justice; all his products are guaranteed to last- never out of date, rust proof. All that he makes and does is honest and true: He paid the ransom for his people, he ordered his covenant kept forever. He's so personal and holy, worthy of our respect. The good life begins in the fear of God- Do that and you'll know the blessing of God. His Halleluiah lasts forever!

We minister to the Lord through our praise and by taking the time to acknowledge his greatness as our experience. It is good to thank him for what he has done, for what he is doing, as well as for what he will do. Our praise should be a time when we boast of him as our God and talk of his excellence, and acknowledge and share these things with one another. When we do so everyone around will be greatly encouraged, and built up in their faith in this mighty God.

Testifying about all that he has done for us personally keeps our every day faith in him real and in the present. His goodness becomes so tangible, that it can touch the hardest heart and be felt by those who are blessed, as well as by everyone else around them.

Psalm Chapter 22 Verses 3
But you are holy, o you who dwell in the holy place where the praises of Israel are offered.

When we minister to the Lord through our praise he rewards us with his tangible presence where we feel and sense him. During those moments he becomes more real to us than ever. Our praise attracts him and extends an open invitation to come and be close and have fellowship with us. Our praise basically makes him feel welcome.

SECTION TWO:

THROUGH OUR WORSHIP:

WORSHIP - This involves paying honour to God.

1 Chronicles Chapter 16 Verse 29
Ascribe to the Lord the glory due his name. Bring an offering and come before him, worship the Lord in the beauty of holiness an in holy array.

What we have with the Lord is all about relationship. Through our worship we respond to God because of who he is. It is the time to tell him how much he means to you and to express to him how you feel about him. It is a time of appreciation where you tell him how what you share with him, is worth everything to you. It is also the time to give him something. It is worth bearing in mind that the thing he wants the most from us is actually us. So when we give him ourselves we're giving him the best thing we could give to him. We can start by giving him our time, our money, basically everything we have and all that we are. However we must be motivated by one thing only, our love for him. Nothing less will do. It is an all or nothing deal. If we were invited to dine with a king or queen, we would not just present ourselves anyhow, with any old attitude or wearing any old clothes. The chances are we would be on our best behaviour and put on our Sunday best. Now imagine meeting someone so much more important! When meeting Jesus we are actually meeting the king of all kings and the Lord of Lords! When we come to God, we must therefore offer and give him our very best.

Worship is the time to be still physically, mentally and emotionally... and to focus on what we know of the Lord, considering all that he is. At this point it is best to forget what everyone else is doing. This is not about whatever else maybe going on in your life. It is the time to put aside every problem, circumstance, and distraction and to focus on the Lord.

Psalm 42 Verse 7
Roaring deep calls to roaring deep at the thunder of your Waterspouts; all your breakers and your rolling waves have gone over me.

We need to look totally to him, enabling him to touch and fill every fibre of our beings with his spirit. There is a part of our hearts that can be found in the very depths of our beings. This part of us belongs only to him and was only ever meant for him. It is from this place that we are to worship him, offering him absolutely everything. This pleases and blesses him as he takes pleasure in his people, and created us for this very purpose.

2nd Chronicles Chapter 7 Verse 1 & 2
When Solomon finished praying, a bolt of lightning out of heaven struck the whole burned offering and sacrifices and the glory of God filled the temple. The glory was so dense that the priests couldn't get in God so filled the temple that there was no room for the priests! When all Israel saw the fire fall from heaven and the glory of God fill the temple, they fell on their knees, bowed their heads and worshipped, thanking God: Yes! God is good! His love never quits!

Our worship and adoration bring the Lord's glory and presence closer.

SECTION THREE:

THROUGH ALLOWING HIM TO GIVE TO US

Psalm 23 Verse 1:
The Lord is my Shepherd to feed, guide, and shield me, I shall not lack.

There is nothing worse than trying to give someone a special gift when they just won't accept or receive it. The giver receives so much joy when the gift they have given is well received. The other incentive is to witness the look of pleasure on the recipient's face.

As we can see from the above scripture the Lord is our shepherd. If we allow him to, he will take such good care of us supplying our every need. Like any good parent the Lord likes to know that we depend on him. It makes him happy when we look to him to do and provide for us, those things we could never do or provide for ourselves.

When we look to him as our helper, source and only hope, he is moved to rise to the challenge. He enjoys proving himself to be strong on our behalf, and loves the opportunity to prove how much he loves and cares for us.

SECTION FOUR

THROUGH LISTENING TO HIM AND ALLOWING HIM TO SPEAK TO US

John Chapter 10 verse 3 & 4
The shepherd walks right up to the gate. The gatekeeper opens the gate to him and the sheep recognise his voice. He calls his own sheep by name and leads them out. When he gets them all out, he leads them and they follow because they are familiar with his voice. They won't follow a stranger's voice but will scatter because they aren't used to the sound of it.

What we share with the Lord is all about relationship so therefore prayer is a two way method of communication. We cannot just come to God and rattle off our requests as if we are reading him our shopping list. Unfortunately too often we do this forgetting our manners. There is nothing worse than trying to talk to someone who walks off as soon as they have gotten what they needed to, off their chest! How rude and yet we do this to God all the time!

It ministers greatly to the Lord when our times with him are not rushed, but intimate, gentle and lingering. He loves it when we make it clear to him that at this time, we have eyes and ears only for him. He loves it when we sit and wait on him determined to hear what he has to say. He loves it when we think he is important enough. Our God is a God who speaks and he longs for us to be interested in what he has to say. The things that we will hear him say back to us will bless and minister to us and change our lives forever! It blesses him not only when we take the time to hear him, but also when we obey him and do whatever he tells us to do. It blesses him when he sees our determination to follow him wherever he leads, knowing he only has our best interest at heart!

SECTION FIVE

THROUGH SHARING HIS SECRETS

Psalm 25 verse 14
The secret of the sweet, satisfying companionship of the Lord
have they who fear revere and worship him, and he will show
them his covenant and reveal to them its deep inner meaning.

The Lord is Almighty God whose ways are past
finding out. He is unlimited and nothing is too hard for him!
However amazingly, this awesome God in his might and
splendour chooses to share his secrets with those who
are closest to him. He reveals to them whatever mysteries
there are regarding the universe. Why would he choose to
do that? Could it be because we are workers together with
him and he considers us to be his partners? Could it be
because if two or three people agree regarding anything
on this earth, it will be done for them if they ask him?
Could it be so that we are so close to the Almighty that we
can declare a thing and it will be established? It thrills him
to be able to have such intimacy with companions close
enough to share his secrets with.

Amos 3 verse 7
Surely the Lord will do nothing without revealing his secret to
his servants the prophets.

This is an awesome truth! The intimacy that God
wants to develop with us is so that we are so close to him,
that he keeps us informed about all that he is up to, and
doing in our world. He wants to involve us in his business
if we are interested. He also desires for us to work with

him and to have an active part in bringing about his perfect will on earth, even as it is in heaven. Sometimes people make wrong and bad choices. However even when they continue to choose to do things their way over his prescribed instructions, he is still so kind and merciful. He doesn't just strike people down in judgment straight away. Instead he reveals his plans to those who are close to him. The first reason he does this is for preparation purposes. His people then have time to get themselves in order rather than be caught unawares. For instance, if there is an area that is not right before God and displeases him, as he gives revelation, we then have the choice about whether or not to put things right.

The second reason for revelation is so that his people can warn the disobedient, (those breaking his laws) giving them the opportunity to repent and change their ways. God loves people and it is not his plan for anyone to suffer judgment and perish, as a consequence of refusing to listen to the truth. As he reveals things to his people they are in more of a position to be able to co-operate with him through prayer. This in turn helps to establish his kingdom on this earth. We as his people minister to him when we show an interest, and give him our yes as we walk in obedience to him.

Genesis 18 verses 17
And the Lord said, shall I hide from Abraham (my friend and servant) what I am going to do?

The Lord was about to mightily judge two nations (Sodom and Gomorrah) for the evil way they continually chose to live. However because the Lord and Abraham had developed such an intimate friendship, the Lord decided to share with Abraham his decision before carrying out his intentions. Therefore Abraham found himself in a position of serious negotiation. He interceded for the nations that were destined for certain judgment and destruction. Abraham was close enough to God for him to actually take into account what he had to say, as he negotiated with God again and again on their behalf.

Proverbs chapter 3 verse 32
For the perverse are an abomination to the Lord, but his confidential communion and secret counsel are with the uncompromisingly righteous (those who are upright and in right standing with him.

When we are close to the Lord we share confidential communication and secret counsel with him. We can share our secrets with him and he can share his with us. As he reveals things to us we are able to pray specifically and with a wisdom that comes from heaven. A determined closeness to him sheds a light on things that would otherwise be obscured by darkness.

CHAPTER FIVE

PRAYER IS SUPPLICATION

SUPPLICATION: This involves an earnest prayer and entreaty done out of a humble heart.

When we offer up a prayer of supplication it means that we are not just praying generally and hoping for the best, but we are actually asking the Lord to meet a specific need.

Matthew Chapter 7 Verses 7 – 11
Keep on asking and it will be given you, keep on seeking and you will find, keep on knocking reverently and the door will be opened. For everyone who keeps on seeking finds, and to he who keeps on knocking, the door will be opened. Or what man is there of you if his son asks him for a loaf of bread, will hand him a stone? Or if he asks for a fish, will hand him a serpent? If you then, evil as you are, know how to give good gifts to their children, how much more will your father who is in the heaven (perfect as he is) give good things to those who keep on asking him.

This scripture informs us that we have a heavenly father who waits for us to come to him with every possible need. The Lord is a perfect father who not only knows exactly what we need, but he also knows how to give us the best gifts. There is no catch, all we have to do is ask. It really is that simple.

1st Samuel chapter 1 verse 10-18

Crushed in soul Hannah prayed to God and cried and cried inconsolably. Then she made a vow:

Oh God of the Angel armies, If you'll take a good, hard look at my pain, If you'll quit neglecting me and go into action for me by giving me a son, I'll give him completely, unreservedly to you. I'll set him apart for a life of holy discipline. It so happened that as she continued in prayer before God, Eli was watching her closely. Hannah was praying in her heart, silently. Her lips moved but no sound was heard. Eli jumped to the conclusion that she was drunk. He approached her and said, "Your drunk! How long do you plan to keep this up? Sober up woman!" Hannah said, oh no sir please! I'm a woman hard used. I haven't been drinking. Not a drop of wine or beer. The only thing I've been pouring out is my heart, pouring it out to God. Don't for a minute think I'm a bad woman. It's because I'm so desperately unhappy and in such pain that I've stayed here so long. Eli answered her, Go in peace. And may the God of Israel give you what have asked of him.

The story of Hannah is a perfect example of the beauty and power of supplication. Hannah had a need and desire so deep that she instinctively knew no-one but God could help her. (Have you ever been there)? She had a husband who tried his best to satisfy her need with his love and kindness. However she had a deep seated conviction that only an audience with Almighty God himself would solve this particular problem, and address this particular dilemma. Without wasting any more time she humbled herself and poured out her soul to the Lord, weeping with every fibre of her being. She held nothing back from God but came to him with painful honesty. She was such a woman of immense courage that she was not afraid to strike a deal. She therefore made a binding covenant agreement with Almighty God. She had such bargaining power with God that eventually she got what she desired of him. She had mastered the true art of supplication and ended up a woman of great joy as a result!

Hebrews chapter 5 verse 7
While on earth, anticipating death, Jesus cried out in pain and wept in sorrow as he offered up priestly prayers to God. Because he honoured God, God answered him.

Jesus took supplication to a whole new level. He often prayed fervently. As a man he had his struggles because life was always a challenge. He found there was only one way to cope, and deal with such things adequately. The answer for him was always to pray intensely calling on heaven's strength rather than allowing himself to be dominated by earth's circumstances.

He used prayer to present his needs, wants and concerns. He felt so deeply about certain things that he was often moved to tears. With deep sobbing and weeping he humbled himself before God the father. He too knew that only the father could help him, and he leaned on and depended completely on him for all he needed. His main concern and the driving force that kept him on his knees, was the horrific thought that anything could possibly separate him from his father. He desperately needed the awesome loving presence he'd always known. How else was he going to be able to get through each day?

TESTIMONIES OF ANSWERED PRAYER

From the very beginning of my journey with the Lord, I have been very blessed to have experienced the privilege of knowing that the God I have come to know and love, is never too busy or distracted to give his people an answer when they search for him sincerely. In spite of bombarding heaven with prayer after prayer, I have found the Lord God has never grown tired of me. He has always proven himself to be the perfect gentleman and totally faithful. With this in mind, here are some of the answers that have come.

PRAYER ANSWER 1:

My friend Lucy and I were at work one day and that morning she had a job interview. Just before she left I heard the Lord whisper to me, "Pray for her before she goes." I heard him loud and clear but thought, "Lord you could never be telling me to do what I think you are telling me to do! She'll probably think I'm mad if I just go up to her and ask her if I can pray for her!" I protested. Anyway, I knew that this was what the Lord was saying. Just as she was about to go, I took a deep breath and asked, "Lucy, can I pray for you?" I was relieved when she happily agreed, and even more relieved when the prayer was over!

Later on that day she phoned me as she promised to let me know how things had gone. She thought she'd done reasonably in certain parts of the interview. However unfortunately she was also required to write a report which she was not expecting to have to do, and that left her feeling as if she had been thrown in at the deep end.

She hadn't a clue what to write! After the interview she was told she would be contacted possibly the following day or even the day after, about whether or not she'd been successful.

That same evening she phoned me to tell me that they had contacted her with news that she had been successful and got the job. She sounded absolutely over the moon and I was delighted for her as well as grateful to God and in complete awe of him!

PRAYER ANSWER 2:

John and I were colleagues at work and we soon became friends. He was engaged to be married and was excitedly planning his wedding. Totally unexpectedly and at the last minute his fiancé called off the wedding because she'd changed her mind about wanting to be with him, never mind get married to him. He had no idea she felt this way and he just didn't see it coming. John was absolutely devastated and became extremely depressed, so much so that I became concerned about him. He lost so much weight and sounded as if he had lost the will to live and go on.

He confided in me that he thought he would never recover from the trauma of being so rejected, neither did he believe that he would ever meet anyone who loved him for him. He lost his sparkle and the twinkle that he previously had in his eye.

I began to pray for him presenting him before the Lord, and asking him to intervene and turn his life around. I also felt that the Lord wanted me to tell John that he loved him, could help and was the answer to all the questions he had about his life.

As we talked he almost seemed convinced as he said, "maybe it is God I need after all!" Suddenly it happened soon afterwards but certainly not the way I expected! I must admit I had it all figured out and planned in my head, how I was going to lead John to the Lord and it was going to be a happy ending. It certainly didn't happen that way. On reflection I now believe that it is never a good idea to run ahead of the Lord. After all he has his own way of doing things! Instead we need to give him the room to work things out in his own way.

On this particular weekend John went down to his home town for his brother's wedding. While he was there, a young lady called Heather fell head over heels in love with him at first sight. She began to tell others until eventually it got back to John.

At first John couldn't believe it. After all he'd been through lately, he just thought it was too good to be true, and didn't want to set himself up in case this too came to nothing. He tread very cautiously and would not fully commit himself to anything. He had no plans to ever give his heart again, just in case things went pear shaped. The memories of recent rejection were all too fresh.

As Heather persisted and wouldn't go away, John eventually allowed his self erected barriers to come down. His emotions although all over the place, began to thaw and he began to flirt with hope. As Heather remained consistent in her pursuit, slowly John began to allow himself to believe that perhaps this time it was for real. They would phone one another and find themselves up talking all night long. Sure enough all things considered, things became very serious fairly quickly.

John resigned from work saying he wanted to move back to maidenhead his hometown, so that he and his new love could be together. He got a new job down there and they got a flat together within a few weeks. Life seemed as if it couldn't get better.

Many years previously, Heather had been told that she would never be able to have children. However after a few months of this happy couple enjoying a whirlwind romance she became pregnant. Their joy knew no bounds as they looked forward to the birth of their precious and unexpected child.

Jesus is a miracle working God and the above is the result. I continue to pray for John and Heather, so that as Jesus continues to work in their lives they will both be brought to the point of salvation, and recognise that everything good in their lives is a gift from him.

I was reminded of the truth of a scripture in Hebrews:

Hebrews Chapter 4 Verse 16:
Let us then fearlessly and confidently and boldly draw near to the throne of grace (the throne of God's unmerited favour to us sinners), that we may receive mercy for our failings, and find grace to help in good time for every need, (appropriate help and well timed help, coming just when we need it.)

Everything that we will ever need can be found in Jesus. I have found him to be my helper, strength, hope, salvation, friend, indeed my greatest ally! Whenever I have needed him I have found him to be there. He has never once failed me but has always been there for me.

CHAPTER SIX

PRAYER IS SPIRITUAL WARFARE

Spiritual Warfare is very serious business indeed and cannot be taken lightly. It involves resisting the devil as instructed in the word of God at every opportunity, and fighting the good fight of faith. Prayer has a very significant role to play in the whole business of spiritual warfare. It is one of the most powerful and effective weapons that God has given us. It therefore enables us to have victory in this war and equips us to tear down any enemy strongholds that have been erected in territory that belongs to us and our God, particularly in specific areas of our own lives.

1st peter chapter 5 Verse 8
Be well balanced, temperate, sober of mind, be vigilant and cautious at all times, for that enemy of yours, devil roams around like a lion roaring in fierce hunger, seeking someone to seize upon and devour.

The good news is that even though we are locked in a battle, it is a war that Jesus has already fought, won and handed us the victory for. We are fighting to enforce that victory in specific areas of our lives and the lives of those around us. It can be likened to when a landlord serves notice and evicts a resident from their property. If the resident remains after that they are literally trespassing. At this point the landlord is within his rights to involve the law and have the resident removed forcibly.

SECTION ONE

RESISTING THE DEVIL AND FIGHTING THE GOOD FIGHT OF FAITH:

Luke Chapter 10 verse 19
Behold! I have given you authority and power to trample upon serpents and scorpions, and physical and mental strength and ability over all the power that the enemy possesses, and nothing shall in any way harm you.

We have so much power and authority as we stay connected and in complete union with Jesus. When we maintain harmony with Jesus we can defeat the devil every time, as we work with God and enforce our heavenly father's will on earth. This will often involve praying against the things we know are not God's will in any given situation, such as illness, discord, crime, death, children out of control, temptations of every kind, barrenness, etc.

PRAYER ANSWER 3

I sat opposite the Gynaecologist as he delivered his verdict. "Well to be honest Mrs Wilkie there is only one option open to you to deal with this condition of fibroids. That is a hysterectomy," he said casually. However I suggest we leave it for now and perhaps look at it again later on when you are older," he continued indifferently.

I was flabbergasted! "Oh thanks for nothing," I thought in total disbelief. As soon as the words left his mouth I began to reject his report, opinion, and expertise, whatever it was. As far as I was concerned maybe he was admitting he couldn't help me, but thank God my future did not rest in his hands! I began to resist and reject what I knew was a lie sent from Satan to discourage and defeat me. I had only just gotten married and knew that it was within the Lord's plan for my life to have children, as the Lord had reassured me of this. Talk of hysterectomy just did not add up, and although it may have been the facts, I knew God well enough to refuse to accept it as the truth for me.

Shortly afterwards, my husband Nigel and I went on holiday to Nigeria to visit my parents. As my dad is a Gynaecologist I felt compelled to share with him what they had told me back home in England, and to get some advice about my predicament.

"How long did you say you were visiting us for?" he asked. "Two weeks," I answered wondering what he had in mind.

"If you can extend your holiday for at least three weeks, we will sort you out here and operate, removing the fibroids. It is a very straight forward procedure and one we do regularly. It is quite a common thing amongst Afro women, so we're used to dealing with it. It is not nearly a big a deal here as it would be in England," he said reassuringly.

I was excited, shocked and amazed at the implications! The Lord was at work and had this incredible plan for me all along. He made a way for me where there seemed to be no way! At last there was light at the end of this tunnel!

That week I went into surgery and they removed thirty fibroids from my uterus. Some of them were as big as large grapefruits. It was no wonder that I had been unable to conceive after two years of marriage. There had been no room within me for anything else! After the operation I was incredibly sore and a physical mess. I therefore spent the whole holiday recuperating and recovering.

Approximately seven months after the surgery I became pregnant. This was truly a miracle. I was ecstatic but very cautious. It was so soon, and now I was going to have to carry a baby in the uterus, that was still so delicate, sore and actually still healing.

When I was four and a half months pregnant I had my first scan. As the lady showed Nigel and I our baby on the screen, we watched completely incredulous. Then she threw a spanner in the works and upset the equilibrium. She confused us when she said, " and there is the other one." It didn't register straight away what she meant. "What do you mean the other one," I tried to ask casually. "Oh the other baby," she said as a matter of fact. Our lives changed forever as we received the shocking news that we were expecting twins.

My pregnancy was a beautiful one but not one without its challenges. The hospital staff called it a high risk pregnancy because of my age, (I was thirty eight), and had only just had a major operation a few months before. The babies I carried were huge babies considering that they were twins. I was quite anaemic as my body struggled to provide for them. At one point my whole world fell apart because I started to bleed. In my mind that could only mean one thing. I thought I was losing them. I was frightened because these babies were so precious. My heart cried out to Jesus in prayer, because I believed he was the only one who could help me. In response he filled me with an overwhelming peace. I refused to give into the fear and resisted it with all my might and strength. I had people telling me that twins usually came early so mine were bound to. I rejected such information, refusing to accept it as my truth. I didn't care how early most twins came, I was going to carry mine to full term!

I had people all over the world praying for me throughout the pregnancy, which meant that by the grace of God I was able to do what needed to be done and carry my babies until it was time for them to be born.

At thirty eight weeks I had a caesarean and was delivered of two strong, healthy, bouncing baby boys weighing 6lb 4oz and 5lb 14oz respectively. This has been one of my most challenging, but rewarding times of resisting the devil and fighting the good fight of faith. If prayer had not been a way of life for me I would not have been able to reject the lie 'that a hysterectomy was the only solution for me.' I would have been robbed of the miracle of been the mother of twin boys. Even as I write this and share this testimony with you, my twin boys are healthy, strong and nearly nine years old now!

PRAYER ANSWER 4

Nick one of my best friends has always been as healthy as a horse. One day he developed what he thought was the flu. His joints ached and his legs felt heavy and as if they couldn't carry his weight. His wife Pat encouraged him to eat but one or two mouthfuls was all he could manage before pushing his plate away. Pat had to pop out for a few hours, so she made sure Nick was comfortable and then left him to rest in peace.

When she got back a few hours later, Nick was totally unresponsive to her and she could not rouse him. Pat tried hard not to panic as she felt the most overwhelming hysteria rising up within her. She phoned her Pastor David who was also Nick's best friend. From what she told him he immediately advised her to ring an ambulance, and reassured her that he was on his way. As he made his way over to them, he phoned to ask me to pray.

Nick was whisked away to the hospital and immediately subjected to various tests. I could not sleep very well because I was waiting for news. I found myself praying on and off all night because under the circumstances it seemed like the most natural thing to do. As I prayed for Nick I did have an overwhelming sense of peace that all was well. During one of the times that I dozed off, I dreamed that the problem was with Nick's brain. When I woke up, I knew that was the Lord's unmistakable direction and that was where I was to concentrate majority of my prayer efforts.

The following morning as I still had not heard anything, I could not wait any longer and decided to phone Pat to see if there was any news. She told me that the doctors had diagnosed Nick's problem as Bacterial Meningitis, (the serious type that can often prove to be fatal). As I received the news, I resisted the natural urge to worry and panic. I felt a strong sense of peace about the whole situation because I knew that the Lord was definitely on the job, and would look after Nick. I explained to Pat that I had dreamed the night before that the problem had been with Nick's brain and that accordingly the Lord had directed me to pray and fight against what the devil was trying to do, most of the previous night! "Pat, keep your chin up! Nick is not just a helpless victim. Jesus is his healer. It doesn't matter what bad news the Dr's give us, we are going to trust Jesus completely and expectantly wait for him to do a miracle here," I said confidently.

That Sunday morning in church, every man, woman and child stood, to pray out of love for Nick. His absence was a painful reality as everyone's eyes rested on the empty corner where he usually sat playing his keyboard. The love we felt for Nick, became our common denominator and motivated us to stand together in complete unity to pray for the man of God. The Devil was handed his eviction notice that day, and commanded to take his hands off Nick because he belonged to God!

Pat and I spoke every day and continued to encourage ourselves even though Nick remained in a coma. Apparently at times Nick became restless and tried to pull the tubes out. The medical team decided to keep him asleep and therefore as still as possible to give his brain time to heal. I smiled to myself, because to me it was just confirmation that Nick was indeed a fighter and would definitely beat this thing. The Dr's later told us that Nick's body had begun to fight the disease even before they had given him any medication.

On the fifth day, Pat told me that when she went to visit Nick that day, he responded as soon as he heard her voice by trying to turn his head in her direction. We were highly encouraged and continued to pray, as well as praise and thank Jesus for Nick's healing.

As Nick made steady progress and got stronger and stronger, the Doctors decided that they would try waking him up. They were however too slow and too late. That very same morning, Nick woke up all by himself! Those of us who love Nick rejoiced without reserve. We believe till this day that Nick came out of the coma as he heard and recognised the powerful and beautiful voice of his saviour

Jesus Christ, calling his name, and commanding him to come forth, just like in the story of Lazarus.

John Chapter 11 verse 4-7
When Jesus got the message, he said, this sickness is not fatal. It will become an occasion to show God's glory by glorifying God's son. Jesus loved Martha and her sister and Lazarus, but oddly, when he heard that Lazarus was sick, he stayed on where he was for two more days. After the two days, he said to his disciples, let's go back to Judea.

John chapter 11 verse 14-15
Then Jesus became explicit. Lazarus died. And I am glad for your sakes that I wasn't there. You're about to be given new grounds for believing. Now let's go to him.

John chapter 11 verse 41
Go ahead, take away the stone. They removed the stone. Jesus raised his eyes to heaven and prayed, Father I'm grateful that you have listened to me. I know you always do listen, but on account of this crowd standing here, I've spoken so that they might believe that you sent me. Then he shouted Lazarus come out! And he came out, wrapped from head to toe, and with a kerchief over his face. Jesus told them, "Unwrap him and let him loose."

At first it seemed as if Jesus just didn't care about the crisis going on in the Bethany household. He certainly didn't seem to be rushing to help in this emergency. However as the story unfolds and reaches a climax, we see that the exact opposite is true. Jesus cared so much and he actually had a plan, to give them more than just their brother back. He wanted to show them how to resist the enemy, even when he came in the most frightening and the worse possible form, the form of death. He wanted to raise their level of faith to another level, so that their belief in him would change things for them forever. When Jesus got through here, none of them would ever be the same again.

As in the situation with Nick, although the situation was very serious, it was not meant to be fatal. Instead it was a perfect opportunity for a much needed miracle from Jesus to make all the difference! Sure enough Jesus did not disappoint. Resisting the enemy by standing in faith (even in the most naturally impossible situations) will lead to victory and move mountains out of the way. Faith exercised and reinforced through prayer, is spiritual dynamite! This is one of the reasons why Satan invests so much in the business of attacking our faith, chipping away at it as often as possible. Resisting him and standing in faith will often take everything we've got. However when all is said and done and Jesus raises some dead thing in our lives, the results speak for themselves! It also becomes obvious that we serve a God who hears our prayers and answers us.

SECTION TWO

KNOWING THE WEAPONS OF OUR WARFARE

2ND Corinthians 10 verses 4-5
For the weapons of our warfare are not physical weapons of flesh and blood, but they are mighty before God for the overthrow and destruction of strongholds. Inasmuch as we refute arguments and theories and reasoning's and every proud and lofty thing that sets itself up against the true knowledge of God, and we lead every thought and purpose away captive into the obedience of Christ (the messiah, the Anointed one)

We are fighting and caught up in a battle that involves enemies that we cannot see with our natural eyes. These enemies are spirits and therefore cannot be contended with using natural means. It is therefore completely pointless to use a gun or a knife to fight an invisible enemy. The weapons that God has given us to fight with are appropriate, effective and deadly, when used under the direction of God's Holy Spirit. Having intimate knowledge of our weapons will greatly affect the way we fight through prayer. Let us therefore examine each God given weapon accordingly!

PART ONE

THE BLOOD OF JESUS AS A WEAPON

THE BLOOD OF JESUS DEALS WITH THE PROBLEM OF SIN

Isaiah 59 verses 1-2
Behold the Lord's hand is not shortened at all, that it cannot save, nor his ear dull with deafness, that it cannot hear. But your iniquities have made a separation between you and your God, and your sins have hidden his face from you, so that he will not hear.

Sin essentially is breaking one of God's rules/laws. It is a serious problem because it actually separates us from God who is the source of life. Therefore it stands to reason then that if we are living happily with sin dominating our lives, he is not under any obligation to respond to or pay attention to our prayers.

It is important to understand that becoming a Christian does not mean that we instantly become perfect overnight. As a new Christian I misunderstood this and therefore had my bubble burst many times. I struggled so much as I considered the fact that too often I still had terrible thoughts towards others, myself, and even the Lord. I behaved appallingly on many occasions and found this unbearably distressing. Thankfully eventually I learned how it actually works. When I made a mistake and got things wrong, as long as I was genuinely sorry, I could go to the Lord to ask for forgiveness and apply the cleansing power of the blood of Jesus. Basically I could ask the Lord to wash away the 'wrongness' with his blood. He would then wipe the slate clean.

As I apply the blood of Jesus I am washed by that blood. When God the father looks at me, it is the blood of his son that he sees on me. He recognises it because it bought my forgiveness. A very high price was paid so that I could be forgiven. As a result I am well motivated to work hard to be right before God. I don't want to take what he has done for me or what he gives me for granted.

Hebrews 9 Verse 11-12
But that appointed time came when Christ the messiah appeared as a high priest of the better things that have come and are to come. Then the greater and more perfect tabernacle not made with human hands that is not a part of this material creation. He went once for all into the Holy of Holies of heaven, not by virtue of the blood of goats and calves, by which to make reconciliation between God and man, but his own blood, having found and secured a complete redemption an everlasting release for us.

PRAYER POINT

Thank you father God for the precious blood of Jesus. Thank you that his blood sets me free from every wrong thing I have ever done, or will do in the future. Thank you that the blood of Jesus makes every area of my life completely clean before you.

Hebrews 4 Verse 16
Let us then fearlessly and confidently and boldly draw near to the throne of grace (the throne of God's unmerited favour to us sinners) that we may receive mercy for our failures and find

grace to help in good time for every need appropriate help and well timed help, coming just when we need it.

PRAYER POINT:

Thank you father that because of the power in the blood of Jesus, I am now in a position to come boldly before you to present my requests, knowing that you are ready to hear and answer my prayers!

THE BLOOD OF JESUS GIVES PEACE

Colossians 1 verse 20
And by him God reconciled everything to himself. He made peace with everything in heaven and on earth by means of his blood on the cross.

PRAYER POINT:

Thank you father that because of the power in the blood of Jesus, I can now have and receive the very peace that you enjoy. Thank you Lord that this peace is available to us, because we are your people. I acknowledge that it is a precious gift that cannot be found anywhere else in this world.

THE BLOOD OF JESUS PROTECTS

Exodus 12 verse 7 and 12-13
Then take some of the blood and smear it on the two doorposts and the lintel of the houses in which you will eat it. I will go through the land of Egypt on this night and strike down every first born in the land of Egypt, whether human or animal, and

bring judgement on all the gods of Egypt. The blood will serve as a sign on the houses where you live. When I see the blood I will pass over you, no disaster will strike you when I strike the land of Egypt.

In exodus God gave Moses very specific instructions concerning how the blood of the sacrificial lamb was to be applied to the homes of God's people during Passover. Under the old covenant 'the blood' was a token and a symbol of the protection that God had promised his people. The presence of the blood was a sign that everything covered by that blood was off limits to evil and destruction. It was a covenant agreement between God and his people. Whoever obediently followed his instructions implicitly received the benefit of his protection.

The blood and sacrifice of Christ was the ultimate sacrifice and the only one acceptable to God since he died and rose again. Under the new covenant, 'the blood of Jesus' is more powerful than anything else and it stops the Devil in his tracks. When the Devil sees the blood of Jesus, he experiences a feeling of de-ja-vu as it reminds him of when Jesus died. He must have been right in the middle of his celebratory party when he received news that horrified him to his very core! Jesus who he had cunningly murdered... had risen again! This he did not bargain for! This he did not see coming! This he had failed to prepare for! Disappointedly he had to accept major defeat. It remains exactly the same today. He has no choice but to do a u-turn. The blood of Jesus is as effective today as it was when Jesus died. The blood forbids him from trespassing, as anything covered by the blood of Jesus, he has to leave alone! As we apply the blood of Jesus and ask him to apply it to every area of our lives, those areas become victorious, safe and out of reach of the Devil's clutches. Quite simply he is terrified of the blood of Jesus!

At regular intervals I find it necessary and helpful to pour out a little olive oil. I then pray over it dedicating it to the Lord as a symbol of his precious blood. Then I use it to go around my whole house anointing every room, asking him to drive out anything that is not of him. I then seal every window and every door with his blood so nothing evil can get in. How often I do this depends on what has taken place in my home and if there have been many visitors coming or going. (Of course no offence to anyone)!

PRAYER POINT

Thank you father for the power in the blood of Jesus. Thank you for the protection that you give me because of it. Thank you that I can apply the blood of Jesus over my loved ones, my home, my job, my health and everything precious to me. I apply 'the blood of Jesus' against every plan of Satan that would seek to steal, kill or destroy anything I consider mine. Thank you father for this powerful weapon of warfare that you have given me, in Jesus name. Amen.

PART TWO

THE NAME OF JESUS AS A WEAPON

Philippians 2 verse 9 & 10
Therefore because he stooped so low God has highly exalted him and has freely bestowed on him the name that is above every name. That in at the name of Jesus every knee should must bow, in heaven and on earth and under the earth.

The name of Jesus is the highest and the most powerful name there is in all the earth! We will never find a name with more authority anywhere, and miraculously absolutely everything is subject to it. It doesn't matter whether it is a natural or spiritual matter, you will find that everything must bow to that name.

John 16 verse 24
This is what I want you to do: Ask the father for whatever is in keeping with the things I've revealed to you. Ask in my name, according to my will, and he'll most certainly give it to you.

If we ask for something in the name of Jesus the most powerful name there is, and if what we are asking for it according to God's will, (in line with what God wants), we have the promise that God will give it to us. When we pray in the name of Jesus, it is as if Jesus himself is praying and our prayers then have all the weight that his prayers have. The father is happy to answer prayers that bring honour to his son Jesus!

PRAYER POINT:

Father I thank you so much for giving me the legal right to use the name of Jesus. Thank you for the power and authority in that name to deal with every situation I find myself in. Thank you that awesome things happen at the very sound of the name of Jesus.

PART THREE

THE WHOLE ARMOUR OF GOD AS A WEAPON

(DRESSED FOR BATTLE AND EQUIPPED TO PRAY)

Ephesians Chapter 6 Verse 10
In conclusion, be strong in the Lord, be empowered through your union with him, and draw your strength from him, that strength which his boundless might provides.

No matter where we are coming from, and regardless of our status, background, or disposition, we all have one thing in common we are all involved in a spiritual battle. It is a serious battle because it is with Satan the archenemy of our eternal souls. It is dangerous enough to cost us our very lives because he is not playing a game. It is his ultimate plan to utterly destroy us if it is at all possible. This is why we often feel as if we are cursed, cannot get a break in life, or that there is some force working against us. NEWSFLASH! There certainly is! He is a very real personality and evil personified! Sooner or later everyone of us comes up against his opposition. He has one mission in mind... 'our destruction'. This battle commences even as early as when we are in our mother's womb! (The proof of this can be seen in things like abortions and miscarriages which are against God's perfect will)!

Under his command and authority are many evil spirits. They all have orders to do all they can to damage and destroy as many lives as possible.

The scripture commands us to be strong in the Lord. Our best and most reliable defence against the devil is and always will be the strength of our relationship with the Lord. So if that is weak, the reality is that we are skating on thin ice! What we have with Jesus must be as solid as a rock, so that we are in a position to withstand every storm that will come against us! The good news is that a close relationship with the Lord is actually his perfect will for us. Therefore investing in this area will bring great reward.

If we are going to learn to fight in prayer, we may as well learn how to fight well, so that every time that opposition comes, we can boldly say: In the name of JESUS... get behind me! Our God is such a good God that he doesn't just send us out helplessly into the battle. He provides impenetrable armour for us to wear on our spirit (the part of us which is engaged in this spiritual war).

Ephesians 6 Verse 11-12
Put on God's whole armour, the armour of a heavy armed soldier which God supplies, that you may be able successfully to stand up against all the strategies and the deceits of the devil. For we are not wrestling with flesh and blood, contending only with physical opponents, but against the despotisms, against the powers, against the master spirits who are the world rulers of this present darkness, against the spirit forces of wickedness in the heavenly supernatural sphere.

This scripture tells us to put on the armour, indicating that this putting on of the armour is actually our responsibility. God has done his job and provided the armour for us. We must do our part and put it on!

PRAYER POINT:

Father please show me how to put on the full armour daily in the proper way, so that I can fight in prayer effectively in Jesus name.

Before we work out how we put on the armour, we need to look at each piece and see how it all connects together.

THE HELMET OF SALVATION

Ephesians 6 verse 17
And take the helmet of salvation and the sword and the sword that the spirit wields, which is the word of God.

The reason we need to take the helmet of salvation is because if we neglect to do so and then step out into the heat of the battle, we will get our head's shot off! It doesn't take a genius to work out that without our heads, the battle is pretty much over!

Bearing that in mind, it is completely pointless putting the armour on if we have not received and accepted the new contract in Christ. This involves the heritage made possible by Jesus' will. (When a person dies their will comes into effect). So we need to accept the salvation that Christ died and rose to gives us. Putting on the helmet of salvation means personally accepting Jesus, and making a conscious decision to pray this way:

PRAYER POINT:

Yes father I want you to be the Lord of my life. I'm sorry for all the wrong things I have done! I gratefully receive your salvation, (freedom from the enemy's grasp) and all that you are offering me. I thank you for the hope that all things good, are coming my way and I now at last for the first time in my life I have a chance to have a great life!

How do we keep our helmet on? There will be times when our minds unfortunately will wonder off here, there, and everywhere. At such times it will be very hard to stay focused on what is the prayer task at hand. During such times it is important to grasp the truth of 2nd Corinthians 10 verse 5 and turn it into a prayer:

PRAYER POINT:

Lord as I cannot just allow thoughts to come into my mind and go as they please, I ask you to help me filter every thought that I have as I am praying. If it does not line up with your word, please help me to reject it immediately. Help me to always know the difference in Jesus name, amen.

Romans 12 verse 2
Do not be conformed to this world this age, fashioned after and adapted to its external, superficial costumes, but be transformed changed by the entire renewal of your mind, by its new ideals and its new attitude so that you may prove for yourselves what is good and acceptable and perfect will of God, even the thing which is good and acceptable and perfect in his sight for you.

PRAYER POINT:

Lord as life may have caused my thinking patterns to become negative and destructive, please help me to relearn the thinking process. Help me to think the way you do more and more. Help me to develop the mind-sets that you have, because your word says that I have the mind of Christ! Lord remind me always that I can do all things through you, and can therefore pray and make tremendous difference to the world I live in, amen.

We have to embrace scriptures like, 'I can do all things through Christ and reject the defeatist attitude that we often have. As we grow and develop in our prayer lives, this must become second nature to us so that in a crisis we do this automatically.

THE BELT OF TRUTH

Ephesians 6 verse 14
Stand therefore hold your ground, having tightened the belt of truth around your loins and having put on the breastplate of integrity and moral rectitude and right standing with God.

The belt of truth is a vital piece of armour because it holds and keeps the rest of the armour in place. If we do not tighten it up in preparation for the battle, the rest of the armour will fall off, and be unable to carry out its protective function. As we tighten this belt, we stand a much better chance in our defence against the many lies that the enemy uses to assault us. The more we familiarise ourselves with the truth of God's word, the more we will be able to hold on to it when we experience the heat of the battle. The battle is designed to persuade us to give in to the temptation to believe a lie instead.

It also enables us to be able to differentiate between those things that are just facts, as opposed to the things that are actually true. For instance it may indeed be a fact that one is sick. However the truth is that Jesus paid in full the price for healing. So it is possible to pray for and believe that you can receive complete healing. So even if the devil were to lie and threaten, "you are so ill you are going to die," the child of God has the option of rejecting such a lie by choosing to believe God's truth instead.

1st peter chapter 2 verse 24
He personally bore our sins in his body on the tree as on an altar and offered himself on it, that we might die to sin, and live to righteousness. By his wounds you have been healed.

John chapter 14 verse 6
Jesus said to him, I am the way and the truth and the life; no one comes to the father except by through me.

PRAYER POINT:

Father as Jesus is my absolute source of truth, help me to reject anything that does not line up with him, or that is contrary to all that I have come to know of him. Remind me always that if I want to know what truth looks like, all I have to do is look at Jesus. Help me to live truth every second of every day, as I familiarise myself with the truth of your word. Help me to pray according to the truth that you reveal to me, in Jesus name, Amen.

THE BREASTPLATE OF RIGHTEOUSNESS

Ephesians chapter 6 verse 14
Stand therefore hold your ground, having tightened the belt of truth around your loins and having put on the breastplate of integrity and of moral rectitude and right standing with God.

The breastplate of righteousness is a covering that protects the heart, from all the fiery darts of life that are often thrown to fatally wound and damage. It symbolises our covenant relationship with the Almighty God through Jesus Christ, and all that this relationship embodies. It ensures that we live safely and with the ability to conquer every foe. This depends heavily on how we live our lives on a practical level, according to the standard God sets, and therefore how right our hearts are before him.

PRAYER POINT:

Father, search my heart and deal with anything that could come between us. Help me to live a clean life that pleases you. Thank you for the victory that such a life brings and that you have given to me, in Jesus name.

PEACE

Ephesians 6 Verse 15
And having shod your feet in preparation to face the enemy with firm footed stability, the promptness and the readiness produced by the good news of the gospel of peace.

Peace does not mean that there are no problems or challenges in your life. Rather peace means that the inner turmoil subsides enough for us to cope and deal with whatever comes. It means that no matter what happens, the inner tranquillity remains undisturbed. The battle to overcome every obstacle and meet every challenge head on is won and every enemy is defeated.

PRAYER POINT:

Thank you father for the peace that comes through being saved by Jesus. Thank you for the knowledge that you deal with every wrong and disturbing aspect of my life. Thank you for the peace that comes from knowing that you know exactly what you are doing, and you know how to fix every broken part of me! Thank you for the peace that you give me that guards my heart and mind, even when crazy things are happening all around me! Amen.

FAITH

Ephesians chapter 6 verse 16
Lift up over all the covering shield of saving faith, upon which you can quench all the flaming missiles of the wicked one.

The trust in God that we have and develop continually, works as a shield and barrier against anything that life would throw at us. Learning to depend on our faith in God can be difficult. It will mean relinquishing the right to be in complete control of everything in our lives, and willingly handing over that control to God. That won't be easy especially as we are a very independent society, and believe strongly in singing the song, 'I did it my way!' Allowing ourselves to become vulnerable to God and totally dependent on him, will take practice and the uttermost perseverance, until it becomes a way of life. This just does not come naturally to us!

PRAYER POINT:

Father thank you for your word that tells me that you are faithful. Thank you Lord that you strengthen me and put me on a firm foundation guarding me from all harm. Thank you Lord that whatever situation I find myself in, there is a promise in your word that totally applies to my situation. Therefore I can stand in confidence knowing that you are able and willing to help me, and that victory is your gift to me. I thank you in Jesus name. Amen.

Matthew chapter 17 verse 20
He said to them, because of the littleness of your faith (that is your lack of firmly relying trust) For truly I say to you, if you have faith that is living like a grain of mustard seed, you can say to this mountain, move from here to yonder place, and it will move, and nothing will be impossible to you.

There is nothing that faith cannot do! We are told in God's word that with God all things are possible. If we choose to believe that there is nothing that we cannot do, we will be able to trample on every serpent and scorpion and have power over all the power of the enemy. We will be able to resist him and he will have to flee from us in Jesus name!

THE WORD OF GOD

Ephesians chapter 6 v 17

God's word is an indispensable weapon.

The word of God is the sword that our spirit man is to use to aggressively attack, hinder, stop and deal effectively with Satan. It is pretty useless to argue with him on a natural or intellectual level as we can see from what happened to Eve in the garden of Eden.. Genesis chapter 3. The undisputed weapon that defeats him every time is the knowledge and correct use of the word of God. When Jesus went through his temptation period in the wilderness, he didn't waste his time having a long conversation with Satan. He just used the word of God to counter attack every lie that was presented. He was successful in the battle because he knew and used the word, and was able to stand on it in the midst of the crisis!

We will do well to follow his example. For instance, on a day where we feel low, depressed and as if there is no point to anything, we can rise up and declare, "I am wonderfully and fearfully made! The Lord loves me and has great plans for my life!"

It is always good to read, study and meditate on God's word regularly, so that we become familiar with it. There is no point when you suddenly find yourself in the heat of the battle, to start having a panic attack, because the enemy is in your face and you cannot find your sword!

PRAYER POINT:

Thank you father that your word is powerful and sharper than any two edged sword. Thank you that your word is the truth and when I know the truth in any given situation, I am truly free! Thank you that your word is the powerful anchor for my soul, when the wind of life decides to blow against me. Thank you that you have made me a promise in your word about everything that could possibly affect me. Thank you that your word leaves no stone unturned. Thank you that praying your word is powerful enough to change circumstances and life itself! In Jesus name, I thank you.

PRAYER

Ephesians chapter 6 Verse 18
Prayer is essential in this ongoing warfare.

This scripture is telling us that prayer must become much more than just something we do sometimes. In order to pray effectively and to enjoy answered prayer, it is vital to be clothed fully in the armour of God and to realise that this has to become a lifestyle. When each piece of our armour is on and in its place, then we are ready and equipped for the battle in the spirit world. Only then can we fight a good fight through prayer and enjoy the freedom Jesus paid such a high price to give us.

In the name of Jesus.... Let us arise and say what David said in:

Psalm Chapter 18 Verses 37-39
I pursued my enemies and over took them, neither did I turn again till they were consumed. I smote them so that they were not able to rise, they fell wounded under my feet. For you have girded me with strength for the battle, you have subdued under me and caused to bow down those who rose up against me.

PART FOUR

FASTING AS A WEAPON

Matthew chapter 17 verses 18-19, 21
And Jesus rebuked the demon, and it came out of him, and the boy was cured instantly. Then the disciples came to Jesus and asked privately, why could we not drive it out? But this kind does not go out except by prayer and fasting.

Fasting is a powerful spiritual weapon especially as it is one of those weapons of ours that is not carnal (natural), but it is a mighty weapon through God to pull down strongholds. In this case a stronghold refers to an area in our lives where the enemy (the devil) has been able to take advantage of us. Somewhere along the line he has been able to gain entry into our lives through a 'doorway' that has been opened. After fortifying the area with his evil negative stuff, he is able to operate from here successfully oppressing us, so that we are unable to enjoy the freedom and abundant life God intends for us to have. The opposition is so strong sometimes that it requires concentrated spiritual focus, and the power generated through fasting to be able to tear it down, resist and remove it completely! With God all things are possible, so even the most stubborn problems, challenges, or strongholds can be dealt with by the power of Jesus Christ, made available to us through him.

Isaiah Chapter 58 verse 6-7, 9-10,
This is the kind of fast day I'm after: to break the chains of injustice, get rid of exploitation in the workplace, free the oppressed, cancel debts. What I'm interested in is seeing you do

this; sharing your food with the hungry, inviting the homeless poor into your homes, putting clothes on the shivering ill clad being available to your own families. Do this and the lights will turn on, and your lives will turn around at once. Your righteousness will pave your way. The God of glory will secure your passage. Then when you pray, God will answer. You'll call out for help and I'll say, here I am.

Fasting works on the basis that an exchange is made in the spirit world. As we make a sacrifice giving up certain things in the natural realm, we are able to receive and gain certain things in the spirit realm. Fasting often has a way of positively affecting our faith. This then enables us to focus more effectively on the things that really matter and whatever it is we need from heaven. Fasting helps to break the chains that captivate, and at the same time release the blessings of Heaven on earthly situations.

When the principle of fasting is done in the way and order that God ordained, and when applied to tear down problems on behalf of someone else, (so the oppressed can go free) it is particularly powerful. Perhaps it is because it mirrors the sacrifice and example that Jesus gave us to follow. He suffered and gave his best for the sake of others. When we fast on behalf of someone else, we are suffering and giving up our plenty to identify with that person, knocking on heaven's door with them. It is a practical example of bearing another's burden, just as Jesus did.

PART FIVE

THE SWORD OF THE SPIRIT AS A WEAPON

Psalm 119 verse 140
Your word is very pure (tried and well refined); therefore your servant loves it.

Proverbs chapter 30 verse 5
Every word of God is tried and purified; He is a shield to those who trust and take refuge in him.

One of the most powerful weapons that we have to combat the continuous assaults of the enemy is the word of God. It is so effective that its application or lack of it, literally means the difference between life and death! It really is that serious.

The more we understand about the word of God, the more able we will be to stand on it as a sure foundation for our lives. We will be able to choose it over and above everything else, as our preferred option.

Unfortunately the reality is that we live in a fallen world. Therefore it is inevitable that most things in our lives (even the most noble) will be contaminated in one way or another. The word of God is however completely different. It is in a class of its own, and it is purity in its highest form. In a contaminated world, full of impurities it is a refreshing change and literally 'A God Send!' Choosing to declare the word of God over our lives is the antidote that removes every trace of anything impure, contaminated, dirty or untrue. Standing on a scripture promise enables every failing and weak area to become clean, wholesome, and full of God's blessings!

God's word speaks for itself and has always stood the test of time. Those who choose it as the foundation of their lives, allowing themselves to depend on it as the most vital thing they have, will find that God himself shields them from the storms of life. They can truly take refuge in their relationship with him. This does not mean they are suddenly immune to life's pain, rather it means they are no longer desperately alone, trying to cope in vain with the latest disastrous whirlwind!

Psalm 138 verse 2
I will worship toward your holy temple and praise your name for your loving kindness and for your truth and faithfulness; for you have exalted above all else your name and your word and you have magnified your word above all your name!

God is a God of his word. He takes his word more seriously than anything else. Therefore when we declare his word over a situation, he moves mightily to ensure that word and the promises within it are fulfilled and kept.

Isaiah chapter 55 verse 10-11
Just as rain and snow descend from the skies and don't go back until they've watered the earth, doing their work of making things grow and blossom, producing seed for farmers and food for the hungry, so will the words that come out of my mouth not come back empty handed. They'll do the work I sent them to do, they'll complete the assignment I gave them.

When God's word has gone out, (for instance when we have declared it over our loved ones in prayer), it is packed with power. The reason is because God takes his word so seriously, that he ensures that word cannot return to him without having a dynamo effect on whatever the challenge is.

Psalm chapter 33 verse 4
For the word of the Lord is right; and all his work is done in faithfulness.

God's word is the one thing in life that is right! In a world where many things are based on trial and error, or just wrong and evil, offering no guarantees, God's word speaks for itself. It has the power to make whatever is wrong, bow to what is right. That is the effect it has. So for instance, if I decide to depend on the scripture 'resist the devil and he will flee,' then no matter what circumstances tell me, I know that the scripture is the truth and right, so I can relax in the security of knowing that God's word has the final say.

Psalm chapter 33 verse 6
By the word of the Lord were the heavens made, and all their hosts by the breath of his mouth.

The word of God is so powerful and potent that it was all that was needed to create the very heavens. This being the case, the word of God is more than capable of creating and destroying, depending on what is necessary. So when I pray using the word of God as my basis, then my prayers are at their most effective.

Psalm chapter 119 verse 50
Remember what you said to me your servant, I hang on to these words for dear life! These words hold me up in bad times, yes your promises rejuvenate me.

Whenever we are feeling defeated, deflated, and depressed because life has battered us and is a fight in one way or another, it is good to know that the word of God applied to our prayer life has the ability to impart the victory, revival and life that we need.

Psalm chapter 119 verse 105
By your words I can see where I am going, they throw a beam of light on my dark path.

When the way ahead seems so dark that you struggle to see the way forward or a way out, and the battle with the enemy rages, the word of God can be depended on. It acts like a lamp providing light to show you what the next step should be. Choosing and applying the appropriate scripture promise will enable you to pray appropriately. This will bring victory and you will be able to move on past even the biggest of hurdles.

Psalm chapter 119 verse 130
The entrance and unfolding of your words give light; their unfolding gives understanding (discernment and comprehension) to the simple.

God's word gives an understanding that provides a bird's eye view of the battle field. From that view point, you are able to see the truth and the reality of a situation as it stands in the spiritual realm, rather than just going by the limited view of the natural realm. Seeing things for what they really are and praying accordingly, automatically makes prayer effective.

Isaiah chapter 30 verse 21
And your ears will hear a word behind you, saying, This is the way; walk in it, when you turn to the right hand and when you turn to the left.

God's word gives direction and guidance so you are not left facing the enemy blindly. There is absolutely no need to be taken by surprise. God's word is clear and sure and brings clarity to every possible scenario. So when we need to pray, we can do so wisely and confidently.

Isaiah chapter 40 verse 8
The grass withers, the flower fades, but the word of our God will stand forever.

God's word stands forever, so it is totally reliable and won't change with every wind that blows. Therefore relying on his word in battle, means that you have a stability that would otherwise be absent. This makes it possible for you to look the enemy straight in the eye, and defeat him before he even realises what has hit him right between the eyes.

Isaiah chapter 44 verse 26
He backs the word of his servants and confirms the counsel of his messengers.

When we speak, use, and live out the word of God, he will move to confirm such a word spoken by one of his servants, often accompanying them with signs and wonders. Another example is:

Psalm chapter 18 verse 33
He makes my feet like hinds feet, able to stand firmly or make progress on the dangerous heights of testing and trouble, he sets me securely upon my high places.

Even in extreme danger, God will keep his servant securely, based on the truth of his word. He will fulfil his promise to you. So prayers based on the word will powerfully defeat any opposition or plan of the enemy!

Matthew chapter 4 verse 4
It takes more than bread to stay alive. It takes a steady stream of words from God's mouth.

Man's very life depends on the word of God, so whatever he has to say on any subject concerning humanity is bound to bring the desired victory, when incorporated in prayer. After all, we all need someone who really knows what life is all about.

Matthew chapter 8 verse 8
Oh no, said the captain. I don't want to put you to all that trouble. Just give the order and my servant will be fine.

All it takes is a word from God! It is powerful enough to change everything. The word spoken in faith is particularly effective and it pleases the Lord. It is the recipe for one victory after another.

John chapter 8 verses 31-32
Then Jesus turned to the Jews who had claimed to believe in him. If you stick with this, living out what I tell you, you are my

disciples for sure. Then you will experience for yourselves the truth, and the truth will free you.

The truth sets you free because you no longer have to live a lie. Automatically your confidence grows regarding the truth about the awesome God you serve, as well as about who you really are in Christ. The devil can and certainly does run rings around the person who doesn't know the truth about either. One of our main goals in life should be to become as familiar with truth as possible!

Hebrews chapter 4 verse 12
For the word that God speaks is alive and full of power making it active, operative, energizing, and effective, it is sharper than any two edged sword, penetrating to the dividing line of the breathe of life soul and the immortal spirit, and of joints and marrow of the deepest parts of our nature, exposing and sifting and analysing and judging the very thoughts and purposes of the heart.

The word of God is the sharpest instrument available to pierce the enemy where it really hurts, getting the job done thoroughly. It is also the very best mirror for us to look into. It enables us to really see ourselves warts and all! This can be quite traumatic but it is absolutely essential if we are to allow God to work in us and change us more and more into his image! It is worth remembering naturally speaking we are nothing like him, so it takes a lot to reach the goal of 'Christ likeness!'

The word of God can and should be used to make declarations concerning all issues of life, and anything that means something to us. These declarations when combined with prayer are incredibly effective and will bring about changes in any situation. Let us look at a few examples here for reference purposes.

DECLARATIONS OVER YOUR MARRIAGE

1/ Lord God Almighty please walk back to the foundation of my marriage and carry out all necessary surgical operations, uprooting and destroying every problem in the name of Jesus.

2/ I bind (render powerless) every strongman that has been sent to come and work against my home.

3/ I pursue, overtake and recover my marriage from the hands of home breakers in the name of Jesus.

4/ Lord dissolve and render to nothing every evil counsel fashioned against my home.

5/ Lord let your acts of fire fall on the root of any marital problems trying to plague my marriage, and cut them to pieces in the name of Jesus.

6/ Let every power working against the divine purpose of marriage in my home be destroyed.

7/ Let every power working against companionship and completeness in my marriage, be destroyed in the name of Jesus.

8/ Let every power working against faithfulness and encouraging adultery, be destroyed in Jesus name.

9/ Every enemy …..Hear the word of the Lord, 'you will not break my home' in the name of Jesus.

10/ I bind all powers eating away the determination of my husband/wife….. (Insert your spouse's name)…, to stay married to me in the name of Jesus.

11/ Pray then in the spirit, applying the blood of Jesus over every area of the marriage.

12/ I take dominion and authority over every spirit and influence (not of God) trying to operate through….. (Insert relevant name), and affect our lives and our home in Jesus name.

13/ I declare that greater is he that is in me than he that is in the world.

14/ I declare that he who began a good work in…. insert spouse's name), in me, and in us as a married couple, will be faithful to complete it in Jesus name.

15/ I declare that the Lord shall perfect all concerning us as a couple in Jesus name.

DECLARATIONS OVER YOUR CHILDREN

1/ Thank you Jesus for …… Your (child/children's) name.

2/ Thank you Jesus that he/ she will be great before you and do exploits in your name!

3/ Lord, cut off the flow of heredity problems in the name of Jesus.

4/ I command everything that will prevent…. (Child's name), from being a blessing in Jesus name, to be severed from them and totally shattered right now in Jesus name.

5/ You spirits of rejection, rebellion, dullness, fear, addiction, confusion, bad dreams, anger and any other spirits or influences not of God, I command you to release my child…… (child's name.)

6/ I command any power that wants to convert my child into a nuisance to be completely paralysed in Jesus name.

7/ I command that any and every spirit not of God … release my children in Jesus name.

8/ I declare that no demonic plan shall be accomplished in their lives, and no evil directives shall manifest in the name of Jesus.

9/ My child.......(child's name) will never labour in vain in the name of Jesus. No demonic mission shall be accomplished in his/her life in the name of Jesus.

10/ I declare that no sickness or plague will come upon my child in name of Jesus.

11/ I break every hereditary curse and bondage upon my child in Jesus name.

12/ Lord I pray against unfriendly friends and demonic initiation through any means including food.

11/ I declare soundness, health, and wholeness in their spirit, soul, and body in the name of Jesus.

12/ Lord Let..... (Child's name) be saved, and filled with the Holy Spirit at an early age.

13/ Lord I place my child.... (Child's name) under the protection of the blood of Jesus and surrounded by the hedge of divine fire in the name of Jesus.

14/ I thank you Jesus that my child....(child's name) is increasing in wisdom, stature and in favour with God and man!

PART SIX

FAITH IN ACTION AS A WEAPON

Matthew chapter 8 verses 5-10
As Jesus entered the village of Capernaum, a Roman captain came up in a panic and said, master my servant is sick. He can't walk. He's in terrible pain. Jesus said I'll come and heal him. Oh no said the captain. I don't want to put you to all that trouble. Just give the order and my servant will be fine. I'm a man who takes orders and gives orders. I tell one soldier go and he goes, to another come and he comes, to my slave do this and he does it. Taken aback Jesus said, I've yet to come across this simple trust in Israel, the very people who are supposed to know all about God and how he works.

The centurion was able to really impress Jesus with his attitude of determined faith. This faith acted as the currency that was exchanged for the miracle of the healing of his servant.

Luke chapter 8 verse 43-48
In the crowd that day there was a woman who for twelve years had been afflicted with haemorrhages. She had spent every penny she had on doctors but not one had been able to help her. She slipped in from behind and touched the edge of Jesus robe. At that very moment her haemorrhaging stopped. Jesus said who touched me? When no one stepped forward, Peter said, But master we've got crowds of people on our hands. Dozens have touched you. Jesus insisted, someone touched me. I felt power discharging from me. When the woman realised that she couldn't remain hidden, she knelt trembling before him. In front of all the people, she blurted out her story… why she touched

him and how at the same moment she was healed. Jesus said, Daughter, you took a risk trusting me, and now you're healed and whole. Live well, live blessed!

This woman activated something in the spirit realm by stepping out in faith. She found herself at a cross road. She knew that he was the only one who could help her. She was forced to make up her mind whether or not she was going to trust in the Lord with all her heart, or lean on her own understanding. Everything that had happened to her up to date, was no doubt designed to try and talk her out of going for gold and getting her miracle. All the impossibilities of the situation meant that here was no way she was going to gain victory in this battle, unless she pressed against all the opposition. This was the fight of her life and her faith had everything to with the miracle she received!

2nd Corinthians chapter 5 verse 7
It's what we trust in but don't yet see that keeps us going.

Faith in action is walking by faith (what you choose to believe) rather than by sight, (what you can see as evidence). It means walking by what you know deep inside your spirit, rather than by what your senses or circumstances tell you. It means choosing to go by that instead. It also means standing on God's word even when things don't look very promising, and even before the fulfilment of God's word and promise come to pass. It is the currency paid in advance for the expectation of the promised goods.

Hebrews Chapter 11 verse 1
The fundamental fact of existence is that this trust in God, this faith is the firm foundation under everything that makes life worth living. It's our handle on what we can't see.

To be able to understand the mechanics of faith in action it is imperative to understand first what faith actually is. With understanding comes easier application. Faith is the firm unwavering belief in the reality of things perceived, seen and heard in the spiritual realm, even before there is evidence perceived, seen or heard in the natural realm. What makes faith so awesome and powerful is that once it is grasped, it is so potent that it can literally affect and defy natural laws. Faith is like dynamite and it can be as effective as any volcanic explosion. Faith had an incredible effect on men of old that did extraordinary things, because they had this powerful dynamite at work in their lives.

Hebrews chapter 11 verse 6
It's impossible to please God apart from faith. And why? Because anyone who wants to approach must believe both that he exists and that he cares enough to respond to those who seek him.

Faith must be in operation for the Lord God Almighty to be impressed. He likes to know that those who come to him do so confidently, knowing that he is real and will not send them away empty handed.

Hebrews Chapter 12 verse 1
Do you see what this means? All these pioneers who blazed the way, all these veterans cheering us on? It means we'd better get

on it. Strip down, start running and never quit! No extra spiritual fat, no parasitic sins.

In order for our faith to be active, first of all we must put away anything and everything that hinders or attacks our faith. Distractions, depression, negativity, doubt, fear, all have to be abandoned. We cannot entertain them and live a life of faith at the same time.

Hebrews Chapter 12 verse 2-4
Keep your eyes on Jesus, who both began and finished this race we're in. Study how he did it. Because he never lost sight of where he was headed; that exhilarating finish in and with God, he could put up with anything along the way: cross, shame, whatever. And now he's there , in the place of honour, right alongside God. When you find yourselves flagging in your faith, go over that story again, item by item, that long litany of hostility he ploughed through. That will shoot adrenalin into your souls! In this all out match against sin, others have suffered far worse than you, to say nothing of what Jesus went through, all that bloodshed!

In order for a fair exchange to be made then we need something solid to focus on. That something is a person and his name is Jesus. When it comes to faith in action, Jesus didn't just have to teach about it. He had to live a life of faith that even cost him his life. Sometimes we as his people are tempted to give up. It can and often does feel as if this life of faith is just too difficult and too uphill. In such times it is always a good idea to remember that whatever we go through, we will never have to suffer the way he did, or be as challenged as he was. As difficult as it got for him, he stayed focused, kept his eye on the prize, lived by faith, and stayed faithful to the cause even to the very end. As his people we can look to his life for encouragement. We can look to him for strength, as he really does know and understand what it takes!

James chapter 1 verses 2-4
Consider it a sheer gift, friends when tests and challenges come at you from all sides. You know that under pressure, your faith life is forced into the open and shows its true colours. So don't try to get out of anything prematurely. Let it do its work so you become mature and well developed, not deficient in any way.

Faith in action refers to having the right attitude in a crisis. The right attitude can mean the difference between a difficult situation achieving absolutely nothing and being a complete waste of time, or it being used to bring about the richest blessings. The challenge is to make the pain work for us to achieve great things in the spirit realm.

James chapter 2 verse 17
So also faith, if it does not have works deeds and actions of obedience to back it up by itself is a destitute of power inoperative, dead.

Faith has to be active and operative because if it is not, it is as good as dead. It has to have actions to back it up otherwise it amounts to nothing more than words, which just about anyone can say or claim. Faith applied to a situation, done in obedience to God and out of a life fully surrendered to him, is much more likely to be productive and fruitful.

1st Peter chapter 1 verse 6-7
I know how great this makes you feel, even though you have to put up with every kind of aggravation in the meantime. Pure gold put in the fire comes out of it proved pure, genuine faith put through this suffering comes out proved genuine. When Jesus wraps this up, it's your faith, not your gold that God will have on display as evidence of his victory.

Our faith has to be tested! The fact is often what we think is faith is actually only a sad imitation. Unless our faith is tested, poked and prodded, it cannot be proven. If it is not proven there is no evidence that when it is needed, it will stand up to the task. What is the point of having faith if when you need it, it falls apart and fails you? What's the point if your faith behaves like a rug being pulled out from underneath you?

2nd Peter chapter 1 verse 5
So don't lose a minute in building on what you've been given, complementing your basic faith with good character, spiritual understanding, alert discipline, passionate patience, reverent wonder, warm friendliness, and generous love, each dimension fitting into and developing others.

It is worth investing in our faith because it is the thing that can change us as we begin to apply and live by it! Putting our faith into action changes everything including us.

PART SEVEN

PRAISE AS A WEAPON

2nd Chronicles chapter 5 verse 13-14
The trumpeters and singers performed together in unison to praise and gives thanks to the Lord. Accompanied by trumpets, cymbals and other instruments, they raised their voices and praised the Lord with these words: He is good! His faithful love endures forever! At that moment a cloud filled the temple of the Lord. The priests could not continue their work because the glorious presence of the Lord filled the temple of God.

2nd Chronicles chapter 20 verse 18-19, 22-23,29-30
Then Jehoshaphat knelt down, bowing with his face to the ground. All Judah and Jerusalem did the same, worshipping God. The Levites stood to their feet to praise God, the God of Israel, they praised at the top of their lungs!

As soon as they started shouting and praising, God sent ambushes against the men of Ammon, Moab and mount seir as they were attacking Judah, and they all ended up dead. The Ammonites and Moabites mistakenly attacked those from Mount Seir and massacred them. Then, further confused, they went at each other and all ended up killed. When the surrounding kingdoms got word that God had fought Israel's enemies, the fear of God descended on them.

Praise is one of the most powerful spiritual weapons available to us as Christians. One of the reasons for this is because Satan cannot bear to be anywhere around it. It brings back painful memories of when he led praise and worship before he got too big for his boots, and subsequently kicked out of heaven.

97

When we praise God it causes havoc in the spirit realm and complete confusion in the enemy camp. When things go wrong but we remain determined to praise God anyway, something is released into the atmosphere, and that something is spiritual dynamite! When we praise God regardless of how we feel, what we think, or how it looks, it is truly so powerful. Logically this will make no sense whatsoever, but by faith we need to choose to do it anyway. It will not make sense to the enemy either who is most likely trying to throw all he can at you to discourage you. Using praise as a weapon enables us to keep going! It also ends up discouraging the enemy who at this point will not know what is going on as you stand on God's word. This greatly affects the atmosphere and no enemy can hang around in this electrified environment!

Psalm 149 verses 1-9
Praise the Lord! Sing to the Lord a new song, Praise him in the assembly of his saints!

Let Israel rejoice in him, their maker, let Zion's children triumph and be joyful in their king!

Let them praise his name in chorus and in choir and with the single or group dance; let them sing praises to him with the tambourine and lyre! For the Lord takes pleasure in his people; he will beautify the humble with salvation and adorn the wretched with victory.

Let the saints be joyful in the glory and beauty (which God confers upon them); let them sing for joy upon their beds. Let the high praises of God be in their throats and a two edged sword in their hands,

To wreak vengeance upon the nations and chastisement upon the peoples,

To bind their kings with chains and their nobles with fetters of iron.

To execute on them the judgment written. He the Lord is the honour of all his saints. Praise the Lord! Halleluiah!

This scripture encourages and instructs us to praise the Lord. It tells us how to do so and lets us know why we need to adopt praise into our lifestyle. The end of the scripture reveals how sharp and accurate the weapon of praise is, and the amazing effect it has on every challenge. A life of praise puts the devil on the run and causes him to tremble in his boots. It terrifies him as God comes in all his majestic might to deal with him, and give us 'his children,' victory again and again!

CHAPTER SEVEN

NECESSARY REQUIREMENTS FOR EFFECTIVE LIFE CHANGING PRAYER

The bible (the word of God) assures and promises us that when we pray to the Lord God Almighty, he will hear and answer us. This is his ultimate desire and will concerning us. However the reality is that unfortunately, this precious communication at times is rudely interrupted. Sometimes it seems like we experience an engaged tone, or as if our prayers are bouncing off the walls without managing to actually leave the room, never mind reach the throne room of God! So we are faced with a dilemma. If God's word is true, (and we know that it is), then why is there often such a gap between this truth and our reality?

It is always wise to go back to the word of God, because it has the answer to every question we find ourselves facing in life. As a child of God through Jesus Christ, there is a certain standard that we must meet and some necessary requirements that have to be met before we can enjoy the privilege of having our prayers answered. In the same way, if we needed to call someone on the phone, we would need to have their phone number and dial it correctly. There is no getting around this simple fact, no matter who we are.

'NECESSITIES' TO BE EFFECTIVE

OBEDIENCE

1st John chapter 3 verse 22
And we receive from him whatever we ask, because we watchfully obey his orders observe his suggestions and injunctions, follow his plans for us and habitually practice what is pleasing to him.

I once heard it said, that the highest prayer possible is living the life of complete and unconditional obedience to God. This scripture plainly states that as we concentrate on pleasing him as our main priority, he will give us the things we ask him for, and desire of him.

1st Samuel 15 verse 22 – 23
Samuel said, has the Lord as great a delight in burnt offerings and sacrifices as in obeying the voice of the Lord? Behold, to obey is better than sacrifice, and to hearken than the fat of the rams. For rebellion is as the sin of witchcraft and stubbornness is as idolatry.

This scripture leaves no room for doubt in terms of what God wants from us as far as obedience is concerned. He is not interested in us making sacrifices by doing things just for doing sake. He is not impressed by us doing things out of presumption. He is not particularly impressed when we do things because it is a noble cause. He would much rather us just get on and do the things he asks us to do. He prefers when we actually listen to him. If we choose to be disobedient in any area of our lives he classes this as a serious violation of his laws. In his estimation, being disobedient is as bad as practising witchcraft, and idolatry! It doesn't get more serious than that!

RIGHTEOUSNESS
(Being right with God)

1ST Peter 3 verse 12

For the eyes of the Lord are upon the righteous (those who are upright and in right standing with God), and his ears are attentive to their prayer. But the face of the Lord is against those who practice evil to oppose them, to frustrate, and defeat them.

More often than not, even an imperfect parent instinctively cares for and nurtures their child. How much more Almighty God. He is the perfect parent who has no imperfections or limitations. He watches over his children continually, and is always listening out for them, giving them his full attention.

This scripture tells us that the total opposite is the case, for those people who choose to live their lives without God. When they arrogantly decide they don't need him, they literally shoot themselves in the foot! Their choices ensure that God himself is against them. Answered prayer therefore is an unlikely experience that they will enjoy, unless they repent and have a change of heart, choosing instead to leave their wicked ways behind.

PERSISTENCE

Matthew chapter 7 verse 8 - 11

For everyone who keeps on asking receives, and he who keeps on seeking finds, and to him who keeps on knocking, the door will be opened. Or what man is there of you, if his son ask him for a loaf of bread, will hand him a stone? Or if he asks for a fish, will hand him a serpent?

If you then, evil as you are, know how to give good gifts to your children, how much more will your father who is in heaven, (perfect as he is) give good gifts to those who keep on asking him!

Having a persevering attitude in prayer is a sure vehicle to receiving what is needed here on earth from the storehouses of heaven. It is always worth remembering who we are praying to, and how much he loves us. Bearing that in mind it is imperative to remember that a delayed answer does not automatically mean denial! If we give up at the first hurdle in prayer, we won't get very far on our prayer journey. If however we choose to persist and refuse to give up, literally anything is possible for us. Our God is a good and great God whose deepest desire is to bless and take care of us.

FAITH

James 4 verse 7-8
So be subject to God. Resist the devil stand firm against him and he will flee from you. Come close to God and he will come close to you. Recognise that you are sinners, get your soiled hands clean, realise that you have been disloyal, wavering individuals with divided interests, and purify your hearts of your spiritual adultery.

Faith is a most vital key that unlocks heaven's door, because without it we cannot even begin to please God, never mind expect to receive from him! Faith is the currency to be used and exchanged for whatever it is that we need here on earth, and are requesting from heaven. In the same way you cannot go to the shop without money, and expect to come out with goods you have not paid for.

RIGHT MOTIVE

James 4 verse 3
Or you do ask God for them and yet fail to receive, because you ask with wrong purpose and evil selfish motives. Your intention is when you get what you desire to spend it in sensual pleasures.

If we think we can just approach God as if he were just a big sugar daddy in the sky, (who is so desperate to please us and meet our every whim and fancy), we will find that we are seriously mistaken. Our God is a God of the heart and he operates heart to heart. He therefore searches the very intentions of everything we do and say. He looks way past the obvious and reads us like an open book. When we ask him for something, his heavenly scanners go over us to discern what is motivating our request.

We can be sure that if evil in any of its forms is behind our prayers, they will go unanswered. God is not mocked or fooled nor can we successfully pull the wool over his eyes!

PRAYING ACCORDING TO HIS WILL

Matthew chapter 6 verse 10
Your kingdom come, your will be done on earth as it is in heaven.

Jesus himself instructs us to pray and invite God's kingdom to come into each situation that we are concerned enough to pray about. This amounts to being a part of ensuring God's will is done, and therefore his purpose established in our part of the world.

Matthew chapter 6 Verse 33
Steep your life in God reality, God initiative, God provision. Don't worry about missing out. You'll find all your everyday human concerns will be met.

Acknowledging who God is in each situation brings a power into operation which would otherwise be absent. Recognising his Lordship, wanting his opinion and sincerely desiring what he wants, makes all the difference and changes everything. When we humble ourselves under God's mighty hand, it affects our heart and therefore our attitude before him. Ironically, instead of this amounting to weakness, and us losing out on what we think we have to have, we often end up receiving even more, much more than we actually asked for!

AT PEACE WITH OTHERS

Matthew chapter 5 verse 23 – 24
So if when you are offering your gift at the altar you there remember that your brother has any grievance against you. Leave your gift at the altar and go. First make peace with your brother, and then come back and present your gift.

This scripture instructs us what to do if we encounter problems with others. It is very important to be obedient here, otherwise answers to our prayers will be affected. If we are arguing and in strife with someone else, we will be caught up in negativity. This automatically affects our relationship with God (who is love) creating a rift so that things will no longer be the same.

However life happens of course, and conflict with others is inevitable wherever there are imperfect people. To deliberately stay within that conflict feeding it, is a different matter and a choice that depends on us.

Romans 12 verse 18
If possible, as far as it depends on you, live at peace with everyone.

To try and resolve the conflict as soon as possible and in a godly manner is the order of the day. Holding on to a grudge and entertaining offences will never accomplish anything fruitful or constructive.

PRAYING IN AGREEMENT

Matthew 18 verse 19-20
When two of you get together on anything at all on earth and make a prayer of it, my father in heaven goes into action on it. And when two or three of you are together because of me, you can be sure that I'll be there.

Prayer is incredibly powerful when two or more people come together in agreement to pray about any particular thing. It is an awesome force when this is done in and for his name sake. The reason is because the Lord said it is in this scenario, that he will show up and do whatever his people ask for.

FORGIVENESS

Matthew chapter 6 verse 12-14
And forgive us our sins, just as we have forgiven those who have sinned against us. And don't let us yield to temptation to but deliver us from the evil one. If you forgive those who sin against you, your heavenly father will forgive you. But if you refuse to forgive others, your father will not forgive your sins.

In prayer there is a connection between what God does and what you do. You can't get forgiveness from God for instance without also forgiving others. If you refuse to do your part and instead choose to walk in blatant disobedience, you cut yourself off from God's part.

Refusing to forgive others opens a door to Satan the evil enemy of our soul. It is a green light to him and is like extending a hearty invitation into the private and most sacred parts of us. When we lack forgiveness we give him legal ground to enter into our lives. Resentment and bitterness represent blatant rebellion against God. Such things form a brick wall which blocks the effectiveness of prayer. They act as impenetrable barriers between us here on earth and heaven above. It is impossible to be able to knock on heaven's door, when our actions and choices have caused it to slam shut and move completely out of our reach!

TRUTH

Psalm 51 verse 6
Behold, you desire truth in the inner being, make me therefore to know wisdom in my innermost heart.

In order for our prayers to be answered it is imperative for them to come from a very real place in us. We also need to have a heart that is truthful and sincere before the Lord. The opposite is repulsive to him because he sees all things clearly and is never fooled by anything we say or do!

PRAYING IN JESUS NAME

John chapter 14 verse 14
Yes I will grant (I myself will do for you) whatever you ask in my name (as presenting all that I am)

Praying in Jesus name is like having a signed blank check book with the Lord's signature on it! However the challenge of course is being close enough to Jesus to access to all that is his, and where we have the use of his power of attorney.

FASTING

Isaiah chapter 58 verse 6
Rather is not this the fast that I have chosen, to loose the bonds of wickedness, to undo the bands of the yoke , to let the oppressed go free, and that you break every enslaving yoke?

Fasting is one of the most powerful and effective spiritual weapons that God has given to his people. When he instigated it as a kingdom principal, he had very definite intentions for its use. Therefore in the above scripture, when people tried to use fasting just as a formula, with wrong intentions, the Lord became most unimpressed.

There are certain situations that need the awesome power of fasting to break the chains and tear the strongholds of the enemy, wherever they can be found. Prayer done with an attitude that pleases the Lord is able to achieve mighty things when accompanied by Fasting. When all conditions are met, the Lord promises to answer our cry when we call him!

CHAPTER EIGHT

PRAYING IN THE SPIRIT

(Praying in partnership with the Holy Spirit)

BE FILLED WITH THE HOLY SPIRIT

As we begin to understand what it means to pray in the Spirit, we encounter the magnificence of our prayer language. This happens as our prayer lives unfold and develop. At first we move uncertainly into moments of stammered prayer often punctuated by awkwardness. We find ourselves tormented by feelings of inadequacy, as we struggle not really knowing what to say, and wondering if we are even saying it right. Sometimes we just feel silly because it seems like we are talking to ourselves or that our prayers are just bouncing off the walls, and not making any difference at all! The great news is that regardless of how we feel or what we think, our prayers are the difference between light or darkness at the end of every tunnel! The key is to grasp this simple truth. When we stop struggling alone in prayer and start working in partnership with God's Spirit instead, the burden ceases to be so heavy. Working with the one who knows everything about everything and everyone, literally charges our prayers with 'lift off!' We will then find ourselves making fewer excuses about all the reasons why we cannot find the time to pray today!

Psalm 42 Verse 7
Roaring deep calls to roaring deep at the thunder of your water spouts; all your breakers and your rolling waves have gone over me.

The deepest part of God (his Spirit) calls to the deepest part of us (our spirit) to have communion and fellowship. The Holy Spirit is God on earth who lives in the hearts of his people. Praying in the Spirit is a vital key to obtaining certain victory in prayer. The reason is because when we pray in the spirit we are so yielded to him, that he becomes our focus as we pray. We literally become a co-worker with God himself. If we are going to pray effectively in the Spirit we will need to be filled with and led by the Holy Spirit.

Exodus Chapter 31 verse 3
And I have filled him with the Spirit of God, in wisdom and ability, in understanding and intelligence, and in knowledge, and in all kinds of craftsmanship.

Being filled with God's Spirit means being specially equipped to do a specific job and to serve God in a special way. (In this case, in the realm of prayer.) During this process, God's Spirit empowers his people to do extraordinary things that would be impossible to do otherwise. Here it becomes possible to pull answers out of the spiritual realm into the natural realm, to meet the questions and needs on earth.

Jude verse 20
But you dear friends, carefully build yourselves up in this most holy faith, by praying in the Holy Spirit,

KNOCKING ON HEAVEN'S DOOR

In order to become vessels that God can empower and use effectively, it is vital to have our faith built up. After all it needs to possess the power to move mountains. This process happens as we pray in the Holy Spirit and spend time with him, basking in his awesome presence. This often is the time when Jesus reveals to us personally how much he loves us!

Romans chapter 8 verse 26
And the Holy Spirit helps us in our distress. For we don't even know what we should pray for , nor how we should pray. But the Holy Spirit prays for us with groaning that cannot be expressed in words.

The Holy Spirit is our senior partner. As he fills us he then begins to intercede for us, in those situations where we have no idea about how to pray. As we groan from the heart that he has filled, he groans and presents our desires and yearnings directly to the father. He does this according to what he knows the father's will to be. It is therefore a good and wise thing to lean and depend on him.

THE GIFT OF PRAYING IN TONGUES

Acts chapter 2 verses 1-8 / 12-18
When the feast of Pentecost came, they were all together in one place. Without warning there was a sound like a strong wind, gale force, no one could tell where it came from. It filled the whole building. Then like a wildfire, the Holy Spirit spread through their ranks, and they started speaking in a number of different languages as the Spirit prompted them. There were many Jews staying in Jerusalem just then, devout pilgrims from

all over the world. When they heard the sound, they came on the run. Then when they heard one after another, their own mother tongues being spoken, they were thunder struck. They couldn't for the life of them figure out what was going on, and kept saying, aren't these all Galileans? How come we're hearing them talk in our various mother tongues?

They're speaking our languages, describing God's mighty works! Their heads were spinning; they couldn't make head or tail of any of it. They talked back and forth, confused: What's going on here? Others joked, they're drunk on cheap wine. That's when Peter stood up and backed by the other eleven spoke out with bold urgency:

This is what the prophet Joel announced would happen:

In the last days, God says, I will pour out my Spirit on every kind of people: your sons will prophecy also your daughters: your young men will see visions, your old men dream dreams. When the time comes, I'll pour out my Spirit On those who serve me, men and women both, and they'll prophesy.

The above scripture tells the story about the fulfilment of the promise that Jesus had made to his disciples. As the time came for him to leave the earth and go back to heaven, he had promised to send the Holy Spirit to them. He knew that they needed help to carry out the task he had set them, and the job he had given them to do. The Holy Spirit came to enable them to become effective witnesses for him. He came with power, with might and with awesome style. His arrival was like nothing experienced or seen before! His presence was way beyond their comprehension, and even to this day nothing has changed! He is still completely unpredictable, and cannot be put in a box or reduced to human formulas! He is Almighty God and cannot be fathomed. However to whoever pays the price and takes the time to get to know him, he happily reveals himself to and works in partnership with.

1ˢᵗ Corinthians 12 verse 10
God's various gifts are handed out everywhere; but they all originate in God's Spirit. God's various ministries are carried out everywhere; but they all originate in God's Spirit. God's various expressions of power are in action everywhere, but God himself is behind it all.

When the Holy Spirit came, he filled them in a powerful and awesome manner. This was manifested as they suddenly found they were able to speak in foreign languages, (which they had not previously learned or known). It was so amazing that people present from other countries were simply blown away. They could hear and recognise their own languages and were baffled! The Holy Spirit gave them the ability to express themselves in ways that were simply miraculous.

In the same way, the Holy Spirit gives his people the ability to speak in a heavenly language often referred to as 'speaking in tongues.' Here a person is able to speak in a language that is not recognised or understood naturally, because it has its origin in heaven. Therefore the person involved is speaking directly to God. It is the Holy Spirit that makes the connection possible. Usually you have to dial a number and go through the switchboard to reach a particular extension number. However speaking in tongues can be likened to not having to go through the switchboard because you have God's direct number.

Sometimes I have found myself in the middle of a crisis. Often it has been because I have had an emergency prayer request, and have not known the best way to pray. Or the situation has been so distressing that I have not been able to find the right words in English. I have struggled to express to God what I need from him at that particular time. In such times praying in tongues has been the answer. I have just opened my mouth and as the Holy Spirit has filled me, he has been able to pray through me appropriately according to his perfect will. This is always based on his unlimited knowledge regarding the situation. Here praying in tongues has given my prayer flight, as opposed to it feeling as if it is stuck in traffic jam!

1st Corinthians chapter 14 verses 2-4 verse 13,33
If you praise him in the private language of tongues, God understands you but no one else does , for you are sharing intimacies just between you and him. But when you proclaim his truth in every day speech you're letting others in on the truth so that they can grow and be strong and experience his presence with you.

So when you pray in your private language, don't hoard the experience for yourself. Pray for the insight and ability to bring others into that intimacy.

When we worship the right way, God doesn't stir us up into confusion, he brings us into harmony. This goes for all the churches, no exceptions.

It is worth remembering that when we speak in tongues we are actually praying and speaking to God, so those around us often will not understand what we are saying. It most certainly is not an opportunity to show off! When we are in public if we do choose to speak in tongues, it is helpful and constructive to do so quietly, as we are the only ones who benefit. On the other hand if we pray in tongues and then ask God for the ability to be able to interpret and explain what we said, then everyone is able to benefit!

TRAVAIL IN PRAYER

John chapter 11 verse 33 & 35
When Jesus saw her sobbing , and the Jews with her also sobbing, he was deeply moved in spirit and troubled. He chafed in spirit and sighed and was disturbed. Jesus wept.

Luke chapter 19 verse 41
And as he approached, he saw the city and he wept audibly over it.

The word travail means to toil painfully. It involves painful exertion or effort as when a woman goes into labour and experiences the pangs of childbirth. At this point she will painfully experience intense contractions, and struggle until she comes to the point of giving birth to her child. This is one of the most natural and beautiful things that happens to us as human beings.

In the same way a similar thing often happens in the realm of the spirit. Sometimes during prayer, the person praying also experiences great travail. They struggle to bring forth and give birth to what God has revealed to them in their spirit, so that it is manifested in the natural realm. This involves the God given birth or manifestation of a vision, a dream, and a word of Knowledge or prophecy. This travail is often manifested by intense gut wrenching weeping inspired by the Holy Spirit. Sometimes this is a reflection of how he feels about a person, or a situation. In the above scriptures Jesus wept over Jerusalem, and over the agony Lazarus death had caused to his loved ones. Interestingly, Jesus still wept over the Lazarus situation knowing full well that he intended to raise him up from death. I believe it is because even though our God is all powerful, he still chooses to get intimately involved when we his people experience excruciating pain. He chooses to meet us right in the midst of it. He is eager to prove to us that when we desperately need a hero, he is the one who is right there. When he hears us helplessly calling, he cannot resist the expression of our lips and hearts. When the deepest part of us calls to the deepest part of him, he comes with the whole host of heaven to rescue his beloved!

LAUGHTER IN THE HEAVENLIES

Psalm chapter 2 verse 4
He who sits in the heavens laughs, The Lord has them in derision and in supreme contempt he mocks them.

The above scripture explains how the Lord God Almighty sits laughing in heaven as he watches the devil's desperate attempts to bring about chaos in this world. God laughs and mocks him because the truth is he has already defeated him. The Lord makes his best and most fervent attempts, as nothing in his presence! For this reason sometimes prayer is accompanied by the manifestation of laughter. This reflects the laughter that is taking place in the spirit realm, signifying a victory that has been accomplished. This also comes with an assurance given by the Holy Spirit to the person praying, that this victory is sure and will soon inevitably be seen shortly in the natural realm. The person praying can start rejoicing once this assurance is given because it is as good as done!

CLAPPING

Psalm chapter 47 verse 1
O clap your hands, all your peoples! Shout to God with the voice of triumph and songs of joy!

This scripture encourages us to clap our hands as we shout to God triumphantly and joyfully sing songs to him. During prayer the clapping of hands also signifies victory and can be used in praising God for the victory seen in the spirit realm. This applies even when it has not yet been manifested in the natural realm.

ANOINTING WITH OIL

The word anoint refers to smearing something or someone with oil to indicate they are now consecrated. Therefore when there is reference made to the Lord God Almighty anointing his people with the Holy Spirit, this opens up a whole new world of possibilities.

It is worth noting that when the anointing comes upon someone it is not a question of feelings. Sometimes a person may not necessarily feel anything. On the other hand, at times I remember feeling as if I was being wrapped in a liquid blanket of love! The point is that feelings or not, the experience of the anointing is like no other! It makes a supernatural difference to the anointed person and to all those around him.

James chapter 5 verses 14-15
Are you hurting? Pray. Do you feel great? Sing. Are you sick?
Call the church leaders together to pray and anoint you with oil
in the name of the master. Believing prayer will heal you, and
Jesus will put you on your feet. And if you've sinned, you'll be
forgiven; healed inside out.

In this scripture, anyone who is sick is encouraged to
call for appropriate people to pray over them, anointing
them with oil in the name of Jesus. Anointing them with oil
also symbolises applying the blood of Jesus to the sick
person. This means that where ever they hurt, the healing
and delivering power of God can flow, making that area as
good as new! The promise is that such a prayer bathed in
faith, will bring about complete restoration for the person
as a gift from the Lord.

LAYING OF HANDS

Whenever I have found myself praying for someone I
have learned it is never a good idea to presume anything!
Neither is it a good idea to try to follow a formula, just
because it worked last time! Each person and their
situation is unique, therefore it is always essential to
follow the specific instructions the Lord will give you at the
time for that particular case. The Lord is so wise and
knows each person individually and intimately. He
therefore knows the best and most appropriate way to
minister to them. Based on that knowledge he will lead
you in all wisdom, to calmly and safely deal with that
person accordingly. There are no hard and fast rules and
therefore no set agenda. Each time of ministry is unique

and requires utter dependence on the Lord for guidance. Extreme caution is called for at all times.

Sometimes as Jesus went around doing good, healing people, bringing life and changing lives forever, he often laid hands on people to minister to them and meet their need.

Matthew chapter 9 verses 27-30
As Jesus left the house , he was followed by two blind men crying out, mercy son of David! Mercy on us! When Jesus got home, the blind men went in with him. Jesus said to them, Do you really believe I can do this? They said, "Why yes Master! He touched their eyes and said, become what you believe." It happened. They saw. Then Jesus became very stern. "Don't let a soul know how this has happened."

When Jesus encountered two blind men, it was a question of first things first. He prioritised establishing their level of faith in him. He prompted a confession from them regarding this. It was very important because faith was imperative to receive and keep the much needed miracle. He touched their eyes and declared life and healing to them, and they received what they needed from him.

Mark chapter 1 verse 40-42
A leper came to him, begging on his knees, "if you want to, you can cleanse me." Deeply moved, Jesus put out his hand, touched him and said, "I want to. Be clean." Then and there the leprosy was gone, his skin smooth and healthy. Jesus dismissed him with strict orders. "Say nothing to anyone."

A leper presented himself to Jesus. He started off by acknowledging that Jesus could heal him if he wanted to.

Based on this knowledge he begged to be relieved from the torment of suffering he'd become accustomed to. He was sick of disease and the shame of living as a sub human outcast. Thank God the scripture says that Jesus felt such pity and sympathy for the man, that he reached out and touched him. Jesus assured him that he was willing to give him the miracle he needed. As a result healing indeed took place.

Mark chapter 6 verse 4-5
But Jesus said to them, A prophet is not without honour except in his own country and among his relatives and in his own house. And he was not able to do even one work of power there, except that he laid his hands on a few sickly people and cured them. And he marvelled because of their unbelief (their lack of faith in him).

Jesus went to his own hometown of Nazareth but unfortunately was not very well received there. There is a saying, 'that familiarity breeds contempt' and Jesus certainly experienced this and found it to be so. As he had grown up amongst them, appearing to be pretty normal, they just couldn't accept or grasp that he was actually quite extraordinary. After all, they felt they knew his background and everything there was to know about him. They were offended at the very thought that he might actually be something special. Their attitude was 'just who do you think you are!' Unfortunately such opposition did not provide the right atmosphere for miracles. So he was very limited when it came to what he could actually do in that place. He just about managed to lay his hands on only a few people there. He cured them since they met the criteria for healing.

Mark chapter 7 verse 32-35
A deaf man with a speech impediment was brought to him, and the people begged Jesus to lay his hands on the man top heal him. Jesus led him to a private place away from the crowd. He put his fingers into the man's ears. Then spitting on to his own fingers, he touched the man's tongue with the spittle. And looking up to heaven, he sighed and commanded, "Be opened!" Instantly the man could hear perfectly and speak plainly!

A deaf man with speech problems came to Jesus for help. The man's friends asked Jesus to lay hands on him and heal him. Jesus following the leading of the Holy Spirit and working in partnership with him, touched the man's ears and tongue. After praying he commanded his ears to open and his tongue to be free. The man was healed and never the same again!

Mark chapter 8 verse 23-25
Some people brought a sightless man and begged Jesus to give him a healing touch. Taking him by the hand, he led him out of the village. He put spit in the man's eyes, laid hands on him, and asked, "Do you see anything?" He looked up. "I see men. They look like walking trees." So Jesus laid hands on his eyes again. The man looked hard and realised that he had recovered perfect sight, and saw everything in bright, twenty-twenty focus.

When a blind man was brought to Jesus he laid hands on him and continued to do so until the man could see completely and clearly.

Luke chapter 7 verse 12-16
As they approached the village gate, they met a funeral procession, a woman's only son was being carried out for a burial. The mother was a widow. When Jesus saw her his heart broke. He said to her, "Don't cry." Then he went over and touched the coffin. The pallbearers stopped. He said, "Young man I tell you: Get up." The dead son got up and began talking. Jesus presented him to his mother.

In the middle of a funeral procession, Jesus interrupted the flow of things. A grieving widow with a broken heart was about to say goodbye to her child for the last time. When Jesus saw the state of play, he was so moved by her obvious suffering. In conjunction with his heavenly father he decided that he had to do something about it. After reassuring her and asking her not to cry, he laid hands on the coffin and commanded the dead man to arise! As sure as the ocean meets the shore, the young man sat up and spoke, because he was suddenly full of life again! Jesus mended her broken heart as he did the impossible for her! He restored to her what she thought she had lost forever. He did for her what no-one else could have done.

What a mighty God he is! One touch of his hand changed each person's life forever, bringing back their hope, joy, peace and their very life! The great news is that Jesus has not changed but remains the same as he always was. He is still full of compassion and moved by the suffering of people. So there has never been a more opportune time for his people to pray. Whenever we see a need it is often because he is showing it to us. Sometimes it will just be about us praying about a situation or person. At other times he will require us to lay hands on people, when we pray and minister to them, just as he often did. However there is no need to become anxious as we try and work out whether we should or not. The more we get to know and recognise his voice, the more we will confidently follow the way he leads us in each scenario. No two times of praying are the same, so it is useless trying to depend on a formula. This is actually a safety net for us. It ensures that in each situation that arises, there is no opportunity for self reliance and pride. It is always worth remembering that without God, we cannot do anything or actually achieve anything worthwhile. Instead we always need to acknowledge the Holy Spirit our senior partner, and our utter dependence on him. We need to be child-like in our trust of him, learning to rely on him completely. After all he has the key to each precious life we encounter!

PROPHETIC PRAYING

Prophetic praying occurs when God gives his child the gift of prophecy. Having this gift enables you to hear clearly the voice of the Holy Spirit (who just happens to know everything about the person being prayed for). Now when you pray according to what God's Spirit has revealed, it deals with the need, brings about the answer, and allows you to speak positively regarding the future. Basically you are now in a position to declare the perfect will of God into the situation. Having divine inspiration, you become able to accurately interpret scripture, (the word of God in the Bible), applying it directly to whatever the situation is in that life. As a prayer warrior you are anointed to boldly speak the word of God, over whoever you are praying for. You have the authority to speak life and truth into that person's destiny. As God sends assurance and confirms his word to the person being prayed for, they are able to relax regarding the situation. There comes a confidence in knowing that they have heard from God, and he himself will establish and fulfil his word in their life.

As the anointing of God's Spirit flows, often he will reveal future events that are perfectly in line with his word, and according to his will. He does this to encourage his people and increase their faith. He wants them to look forward to the good plans he has for them, and eagerly anticipate them being fulfilled. God wants his children to be left strengthened, and ready to meet the terms and conditions required. He wants them to actively do their part by using their faith to receive his richest blessings!

Isaiah chapter 38 verses 4-6
Then God told Isaiah, go and speak with Hezekiah. Give him this message from me, God, "I've heard your prayer. I have seen your tears. Here's what I'll do: I'll add fifteen years to your life. And I'll save both you and this city from the king of Assyria.

King Hezekiah was ill and dying. He was however unhappy with the verdict, and prayed to get the outcome changed. God in his mercy heard his heartfelt prayer and decided to grant his request of an extension to his life.

Isaiah the prophet was on hand to speak a much needed word from God into the situation. He no doubt brought clarity and reassurance as well as a prophetic word, regarding what was to take place during Hezekiah's lifetime.

Luke chapter 2 verse 25-28 32-35
In Jerusalem at the time, there was a good man called Simeon. He lived in the prayerful expectancy of help for Israel. And the Holy Spirit was on him and intimately involved with him. The Holy Spirit had therefore shown him that he would see the messiah of God before he died. Led by the Spirit he entered the temple. As the parents of Jesus brought him to carry out the rituals of the law, Simeon took him in his arms and blessed God: Joseph and his mother were speechless with surprise at the man's words. He began to prophecy regarding Jesus, and the future events concerning him. Mary and Joseph marvelled at the things that were said about their little boy. This must have really confirmed just how special their baby was, and what an awesome destiny he was born for, and had ahead of him. Simeon went on to bless them, and said to Mary his mother, "This child marks both the failure and the recovery of many in Israel, A figure misunderstood and contradicted, the pain of a sword thrust through you. But the rejection will force honesty, as God reveals who they really are."

Luke chapter 2 Verse 36-38
Anna the Prophetess was also there. At the very time Simeon was praying, she showed up, broke into an anthem of praise to God and talked about the child to all who were waiting expectantly for the freeing of Jerusalem.

Just as Mary and Joseph must have been struggling to come to terms with what Simeon had said, Anna a prophetess also came over. She too made a point of thanking God for Jesus. She also shared what had been revealed to her about him.

The objective of a word of prophecy is to let people in on what God is doing. It aims to bring them in line with what he has planned for them. If they are adequately informed they are less ignorant and more likely and able to cooperate. They can get with the programme and get out of the way instead of obstructing and delaying God's perfect will on earth!

CHAPTER NINE

(PRAYER IS RECEIVING GUIDANCE AND REVELATION FROM THE LORD)

We cannot see what way ahead of us is. Therefore it is absolutely vital for us to hear from the one, who can see even around the corners of our lives! It is imperative to remember that we need him because he has the map. Only he can show us what we're supposed to be doing, and where we're supposed to be going! If we find ourselves going down the wrong path, we surely need the Lord. He is the one who is more than able to put us back on track! The truth is he knows the way because he actually is the way. He is the door through whom we must pass, to be able to move forward with our lives.

John chapter 14 verse 6
Jesus told him, I am the way, the truth and the life.

A few years ago I found myself at a very difficult point in my life. Something very bad was happening. It literally felt as if the whole of hell had been let loose with one aim in mind…... Destruction. My marriage was on the rocks and I had begun to try to work out how my husband and I could separate in the least traumatic way (practically speaking). The people I had around me all had an opinion about what I should do, and all offered their ten pence worth! It was as if I had asked them to vote and the vote was unanimous…. End the marriage, leave the husband!
I had begun to imagine what life would be like as a single mum, trying to raise my two five and half year old

sons all by myself. I became completely overwhelmed with the challenge, of trying to work out what I was going to do! On top of everything else I was so confused. Ending my marriage did seem to be the logical thing to do. However I just had a nagging feeling that this was all wrong. Although separation was definitely on the cards, it didn't feel or seem right. I hated the idea of my two little boys growing up without their father.

The pressure of the situation drove me to intense prayer, because I really didn't know what to do for the best. All I knew was that I really couldn't afford to get this wrong; there was just too much at stake!

My prayer went something like this :

Lord I know that you love Nigel and I and our two little boys and you have a plan for our lives. You see everything clearly and you know the issues and problems we are facing at the moment. Lord I am so confused and I don't know what to do for the best. Should I take everyone's advice and call it a day on my marriage? Lord please speak to me and tell me what I should do, because I really don't know. Whatever you tell me to do I will do it. The bottom line is when all is said and done I want to please and obey you; and only you.

LIFE CHANGING ANSWER TO PRAYER!

A few days later I had a dream. It literally shook me up so much that it changed the complete course of my life. I found myself doing a 360 degree about turn.

I dreamed that I went to a place that looked like a wedding reception. Significantly I had gone to the function by myself. I got there a little late as the eating part was already in full swing. People were helping themselves to the food that had been provided. I looked around to see where I should go to get something to eat, and decided to make my way over to the buffet table. There were plates of food already prepared and wrapped in cling film. I presumed they were for people who wanted to save time rather than join the queues. I decided to take one of these plates then I sat down to eat. I put a few mouthfuls in my mouth when suddenly looking down into what I was eating, I noticed that it looked as though someone had spat their saliva into my plate! Obviously initially I hadn't noticed, but as soon as I realised I became extremely distressed to say the least. I knew I had eaten some already, and that it was too late to do anything about it. At that point I woke up and felt deeply disturbed. I asked the Lord what on earth it all meant as I knew it had some major significance.

The Lord gracious and loving as ever was very obliging and soothed my troubled heart. He reassured me with these words, "Child of my love, the food that you ate (that had saliva in it) is symbolic. It represents the advice you have been receiving from those around you, which you have been acting upon. The problem is that for a long time you have been accepting this food (advice) as gospel, but the reality is that it has been severely defiled by ungodly demonic influences. A defiled thing has no power therefore to offer anything good or fruitful. You have been unaware of this because the food has always been presented with the finest cling film on it. It has certainly looked the part and given the impression that it is good for you to eat. However if any of it was truly good it would have helped and healed your marriage, instead of harming it and being a major cause of the problems within it! Child of my love its not too late. Although you have eaten some of this food already, all is not lost. It is imperative that you turn your back on all you have known. Decide now to stop eating 'already prepared food covered by cling film, so to speak. From now on you need to be bold and brave enough to get your own empty plate. Bring it to the table that I have laid out for you myself. Choose and pick whatever you want, instead of what you are told has been decided you must have! If you have any special requests and desires you come directly to me. I will move heaven and earth literally to see to it that you get what you need. I will also ensure that it is of the highest quality and unmistakably beneficial to you. My child, no longer go to people for the answers to the puzzles of life. They don't have the blueprint for their own life never mind yours! Yes they may have a few pieces of the puzzle but not enough for them to qualify to run the whole show! On the other hand, there is nothing that is too hard for me and there is nothing I cannot do! I love you and will spend the rest of your life proving to you just how much. If you will trust me in this, you'll see that I will never fail or disappoint you.

Ephesians chapter 3 verse 20
Now glory be to God! By his mighty power at work within us, he is able to accomplish infinitely more than we would ever dare to ask or hope.

He continued, " In answer to your question it is not my perfect will for you and Nigel to separate and for your marriage to fail. Remember I brought the two of you together! Therefore if you are willing to trust and work with me, we can repair whatever is broken in your marriage. I warn you however that the kingdom of hell won't like it and just roll over and play dead. You are going to have to fight to regain lost territory. Don't be afraid though because I will be with you. The strategy that we will use to fight is the most powerful weapon that exists. It is the weapon of love. Love has the power to break every chain and stronghold, and at the same time bring every enemy to its knees. There is nothing that is impossible for me to achieve! So if you choose to obey me in this, disregard and ignore all other advice (coming from the enemy's camp and chief advisers), then I will give you the type of marriage that most folk only dream about but never manage to obtain! I want you to start now and don't lose another second….. Love your husband like never before. Enable and allow him to know my love through you, in a way he has never managed to experience before! This is my perfect plan for your marriage!" he concluded.

I almost fainted with relief and shock that this didn't have to be the end of us, as a couple and as a family! I took all that he said to me very seriously holding it close to my heart, like a nervous child does with their favourite comfort blanket. As a result this was the beginning of the end of many things in my life. The Lord took me on a life changing journey. Everything including every single relationship in my life up to that date, had to go under the Lord's microscope to be ruthlessly scrutinised. The Lord showed me every source of poison which was truly a shocking experience! The poison was coming from places I would never have dreamt of. This was the reason why it had been possible for me to be deceived in the first place!

I learned that I had to stop feeding every root, dig them all up and leave them to die. Anything that was not of God in my life had to go, regardless of the personal cost or how much it would hurt. It turned out to be one of the most painful experiences of my life. I felt like I was literally cutting off my own limbs! However it had to be done because if poison is not dealt with quickly it kills everything in its path. Thank God on this occasion its intention had been frustrated. It had failed to kill my marriage!

One of the most important things that prayer helped me to realise and understand was that although the poison came through people, most of the people involved were not actually bad people. It was just that they had issues that they failed to surrender and allow God to help them deal with. This affected their motives and intentions making them questionable. As a result unfortunately these things became their weaknesses, making them perfect candidates to be exploited and used by the devil for his purposes (basically whatever was the opposite to what God wanted).

I share this next story to show just how the devil works to cause harm. The lack of prayer on my part gave him the green light to be able to do so!

I met a young lady called Brenda. Before long she became a close friend of mine, and in the end I actually considered her to be more like a sister to me. Brenda had been through the mill, because as a child she experienced one tragedy after another. First she lost her father in a car accident, and before she could recover she lost her mother to cancer two years later. By the time Brenda became a teenager, she was an angry young woman with one or two major issues to say the least. She developed certain methods of self preservation which included the art of manipulation. The result was that she would fly off the handle whenever she didn't get her own way. She also became an expert at controlling whoever got close enough to her to be included in her 'inner circle.' The people close to her didn't of course realise what was going on at first, as she learned to pull their strings just like they were her puppets. Before long they were all dancing to her music. Anyone who did not agree with her, was excluded from her close circle of inner friends and were basically in the dog house! Those however who jumped particularly well to any new tune she played, graduated to being referred to as her 'new family.'

Brenda thought nothing of willingly choosing to control, manipulate and use people for her own purpose.... namely making herself feel better about her own life! She often put others down if that meant making faster progress towards that end. She also blew her own trumpet in a covert way making everything always about her in some way. Sometimes that meant taking on the identity of a constant victim, so that those around her felt sorry for her and became obliged to keep her feeling fixed! She seemed to enjoy always being the victim, as she received pity, sympathy and constant attention. No wonder she never seemed to want to get over difficult things that had happened to her and move on.

Unfortunately the danger in all this was that her audience were not always human.

Ephesians Chapter 6 verse 10
For we are not fighting against people made of flesh and blood, but against the evil rulers and authorities of the unseen world,

against those mighty powers of darkness who rule this world, and wicked spirits in the heavenly realms.

In fact there were undercurrent forces at work! Brenda's choices had opened doorways in the spirit world. As a result ironically these evil spirits decided to latch on to Brenda and exploit her for their own purposes. They didn't just appear as horned devils (as this would obviously have alerted people to their presence and method of operation much earlier)! Instead they chose to appear incognito (spiritually speaking of course), taking on the slithery form of a snake therefore manifesting themselves in the same way.

Genesis chapter 3 verse 1, 13-15
Now the serpent was the shrewdest of all the creatures the Lord God had made.

Then the Lord God asked the woman, "how could you do such a thing?"

"The serpent tricked me," she replied. "That's why I ate it."

So the Lord God said to the serpent, "because you have done this, you will be punished. You are singled out from all the domestic and wild animals of the whole earth to be cursed. You will grovel in the dust as long as you live, crawling along on your belly. From now on you and the woman will be enemies, and your offspring and her offspring will be enemies. He will crush your head and you will strike his heel."

Check out the full story in Genesis 3 and see the shocking slithering snake in action!

The spirits involved in Brenda's case were the spirits of manipulation and control. They took it in turns to manifest themselves as the snake. It all depended on which one was operating at any given time. Working closely as partners, whenever there was a situation that suited their purposes, they would literally slither undetected in and out of the relationships and lives of the people involved with Brenda. This caused havoc, pain, harm and destruction as they slithered around, putting down venomous poison at every available opportunity. Often this was powerful enough to hijack the relationships, causing them to disintegrate and become a mound of old ruins.

As Brenda had deep rooted issues that had never been addressed never mind dealt with, the spirits found a willing and perfect vessel to use to leave their destructive mark. Before long wherever Brenda could be found, there was usually a trail of devastation and destruction left behind to tell the tale. More often than not it could be traced back to her in some way shape or form. Marriages literally fell apart at the seams, as couples bickered and considered separating due to Brenda's 'input'. People's finances became like a bucket with a hole in it, sicknesses became a way of life to her nearest and dearest, problems arose in friendships, amongst siblings, and the list was endless. Unfortunately for those involved, it seemed the source of the problem was never easily recognisable. Brenda worked over time and under cover, always trying to appear to be an indispensable model citizen, and a pillar of society doing great and awesome things in the community!

Matthew chapter 24 verse 24
For false Christ's and false prophets will arise and they will show great signs and wonders so as to deceive and lead astray, if possible, even the elect (God's chosen ones)

The reality was though, as Brenda became more frequently one with these evil spirits pandering to their every whim, it became increasingly difficult to ascertain where she ended and the spirits began. As a result she literally became like a leech, latching on to and sucking the very life out of whoever happened to be involved with her.

As the spirits of control and manipulation began to dominate her life they whispered into her ears. Making their demands on her, she in turn became more and more demanding of the people she was involved with. Initially she'd only take an inch here and there. Before long however she was literally demanding the whole nine yards, and literally taking over their whole lives. Somehow before they had even realised what was going on, she was demanding to be the first and main priority in their lives. Those who bowed to the pressure found that they literally had no life left to talk about, because suddenly there was nothing that didn't include her. Those who tried to stand up to her had no idea that they were dealing with powerful spirits. They were soon slapped down in humiliation, and left clambering in some corner somewhere, or completely excluded. The weak ended up feeling it wasn't worth risking the wrath of a woman scorned. Wherever Brenda went, the slithering snake would open it's fangs, bare teeth perfect for job and bite people laying down its deadly poison. (spiritually speaking)

To keep those around her in line Brenda often employed the 'apparent kindness' method. Here she would appear to be extravagant in her giving, and it would seem as if she couldn't do enough for the people in her life. However after one of these particular giving phases, she would manipulate them up into a frenzied feeling that they literally owed her their lives. The price to be paid was for the privilege of having her in theirs. She expertly convinced them that she was doing them a huge favour and now they were indebted to her forever.

Jeremiah chapter 33 verse 3
Call to me and I will answer you and show you great and mighty things, fenced in and hidden, which you do not know(do not distinguish and recognise, have knowledge of and understand.)

As my marriage was going downhill fast and felt as if it was literally in the toilet, the help I needed was of an emergency nature. After much prayer the Lord showed me things that initially I didn't know or understand. I prayed because I needed to know how to get my life back! What I didn't know at the time was that my husband Nigel spent time on his knees praying. He cried and sobbed before the Lord because his heart was broken. He had no idea how to get his wife back and save our failing marriage! So he pleaded with God to do something. From the depths of despair he asked God to give me revelation, so that whatever had bewitched me would release me and let me go! He was so desperate for me to snap out of the trance I seemed to have fallen into!

Looking back I'm so thankful that Jesus is the true and living God! At that time we both knocked on heaven's door and the God of heaven, was kind enough to answer two desperate people! He opened the door and gave us access to heaven's resources. Before our very eyes he took our marriage in his miracle working hands. With deepest love he tenderly healed and delivered it completely. He kept his word to me and his side of the bargain, doing things for Nigel and I that I cannot even articulate. The only thing suitable that I can do is humbly bow my knees and worship this awesome mighty God!

The apparent kindness method Brenda used was the same method employed to get someone hooked on drugs! She learned to tell people exactly what she knew they wanted to hear. Many times a drug dealer will offer someone a 'freebie' and allow them to try a drug for free. Once they have tasted and liked the effect, then they keep going back to the same drug dealer, because now they are addicted. Only now they have to pay for the privilege. Suddenly they can literally get the addicted person to jump through hoops. Any usual logic, caution or just plain common sense flies out the window. At this point they are just so desperate for their next fix! They'll do anything and pay through the roof for it if necessary. The person addicted often believes that the drug dealer cares, loves them and is offering them something good, because now the power of association is at work also. To them the drug dealer represents a good feeling, and emotional high, even if only temporary. As a result they soon become hooked on the drug and inevitably the supplier too! The supplier can now call all the shots, make tremendous demands and profit, as well as a nice little earner and steady income. It is a set up from hell, but the problem is now the deal is clinched.

The presence of manipulation also works as an anaesthetic. When the favour, or sugar coated good stuff is offered and given, it works as a distraction to the pain of having the manipulator latch on to your neck (metaphorically speaking). It serves to dull the pain of having your very life being sucked out of you! It works in the same way as offering a child a lollipop when they have been taken to the dentist to have their tooth pulled out! The lollipop is what makes the tooth go bad in the first place because of the (sugar content). However it can be the very thing that is used as a pacifier for the pain and trouble caused.

The only way to gain freedom and to get clean is go cold turkey. This often will be traumatic because it will mean having to move away, (Spiritually, physically, emotionally, and mentally). You may have to use a substitute for the drug, as well as develop a determination and persistence that you may never have displayed before. It will feel as if your life depends on it! The truth is it actually does!

A WORD OF WARNING: The drug dealer and of course the spirits involved are not likely to be very impressed. As a result they won't just lie down and play dead! They will become aggressive towards you, in their desperation to continue to control and manipulate you and your life. If you dare to stand up to them (in the strength and power of God that comes through prayer), and start telling them no they won't like it, especially if in the past you gave into their demands! Hold your head up high though and be encouraged. If you do not continue to feed something, eventually it will have no choice but to die!

A perfect example of this can be found in:

Acts Chapter 16 verse 16-19,22

One day as we were going down to the place of prayer, we met a demon possessed slave girl. She was a fortune-teller who earned a lot of money for her masters. She followed along behind us shouting, "These men are servants of the most high God, and they have come to tell you how to be saved." This went on day after day until Paul got so exasperated that he turned and spoke to the demon within her. "I command you in the name of Jesus Christ to come out of her," he said. And instantly it left her. Her master's hopes of wealth were now shattered so they grabbed Paul and Silas and dragged them before the authorities at the marketplace. The whole city is in an uproar because of these Jews they shouted. A mob quickly formed against Paul and Silas, and the city officials ordered them stripped and beaten with wooden rods. They were severely beaten and then they were thrown in prison. The jailer was ordered to make sure they didn't escape. So he took no chances but put them into the inner dungeon and clamped their feet in the stocks.

The people in Brenda's life were so manipulated by her that they were filled with a manufactured gratitude all the time. This was based on her "apparent generous forgiveness." They became so overwhelmed with it that they could never say no to her again, without her making them feel as though they had to apologise. The unspoken questions seemed to be, "how dare anyone rebel and make a choice of their own which did not include her? "How dare anyone commit the abomination of wanting to be independent from her?" "How could anyone be so cruel after all she'd been through already in her life?" These were the questions that filled the atmosphere. To seal things Brenda made it clear that for the crime of 'hurting her,' they would never be able to make it up to her! They did however have her permission to spend the rest of their lives trying!

There were signs and alarm bells going off early on in our relationship but I missed them all. I loved Brenda and so was particularly vulnerable to be taken for a ride. I couldn't imagine that the feelings were not mutual. When it came to this particular relationship I got caught out because I didn't tread prayerfully. For some naïve reason I never imagined for one second that I needed to. In hindsight however I can see clearly now that failing to do so cost me so dearly!

When Nigel came along and started courting me, problems inevitably developed. As my relationship with him deepened, we fell head over heels in love and decided to get engaged. Often Nigel would visit me after work and we'd spend the evening together. It became apparent that Brenda became more and more resentful as time went on. Before Nigel came along, those evenings were spent having a cosy girl's night in. Now suddenly she felt that I no longer had time for her and that she had been displaced. All of a sudden all her hard work had come to nothing, because she had ceased to be the centre of my world. Often she would drive by my flat, see Nigel's car parked outside and end up feeling more unimpressed. She played the role of the helpless victim to perfection, crying to whoever offered her a shoulder. If Oscars were being handed out at the time, she would no doubt have received the first one. By the grace of God our wedding took place anyhow. It seemed as a result she waited, she plotted, and she planned her sweet revenge. Her intention apparently was to make us pay for daring to be together and have a life apart from her! The slithering snake moved unseen as it hissed with delight as Brenda's face became contorted with disdain. Of course marriage is a challenge at the best of times. However things did start to go wrong for us as Brenda's presence and the sum total of her input, amounted to major interference in our marriage. To be fair it hardly stood a chance as long as she continued to remain around us!

Once I'd arranged to spend some time with my cousin Carol. We hadn't seen each other in a while so I was really looking forward to spending some quality time with her.

Somehow Brenda got wind of it and decided she was going to gate crash the party! She began to ring my phone like she was literally possessed! In the end I actually lost count of how many times she actually phoned. That day it felt like I was being harassed by a crazy frenzied stalker. Eventually I tried to handle the situation because I realised she just would not go away! When it rang again I decided to answer the phone and speak to her. I explained to Brenda that I hadn't answered the phone earlier because I was just having a bit of time to myself. She didn't sound happy about that at all. To make matters worse I hadn't bowed to the pressure she tried to exert. I didn't bother to try to make amends. I refused to invite her to come round and join my cousin and I for the afternoon. I chose to carry on with my plans just the way they were. (Without actually saying so she seemed to ask the question, "How dare you exclude me and even worse not ask my permission to make this choice or seek my approval)?"

The next thing I knew my cousin Carol came round but instead of us having a lovely time together, she actually laid into me and had a go at me. She said, "I just spoke to Brenda and she said that when she spoke to you earlier, that you were being funny with her!" Carol actually seemed angry with me! I mumbled something about my need to set boundaries around my life, but to be honest I felt so intimidated by the presence of the spirits of control and manipulation. I literally found myself retracting what I had started out saying. I backtracked and dropped all charges. I ended up feeling terrible about exerting my right to make the choice. On top of that the time with my cousin was ruined. Brenda had won again and the two evil spirits at work seemed to clap their hands with glee.

It was amazing that no matter what games she played, Brenda always managed to get the world and his wife to defend her honour! She never accepted responsibility for any of the chaos she caused. All she had to do was play the victim and everyone felt so sorry for her. As a result there was never any question of confronting her about anything. Apparently no one had the heart to cause her further pain. In fact those around her were filled with an overwhelming desire to protect the poor damsel in distress! In the mean time the snake would slither off time and time again satisfied with another's days work.

(The concise English dictionary's definition of the word manipulate...... To handle , to treat, skilfully; to manage, influence, or tamper with by artful means.)

Manipulation stands for everything that God is not! He gave us freewill and never treats us like we are his puppets, or just pawns in a chess game! So as people of God how dare we ever treat one another like this and think it's alright to resort to any of these ungodly tactics? The slithering snake in the garden of Eden did that to Eve, and craftily managed to talk her out of her inheritance. She lost her beautiful home, symbolic of the awesome plan God had for her! Do we want to imitate him, rather than the God who has loved us with an everlasting love?

Be honest with yourself before God. Have you ever found yourself emotionally blackmailing someone in your life? Have you relentlessly bullied and stalked them? Have you put pressure on them hoping to manipulate them into doing whatever you want them to do or say? Have you regularly violated their freewill, leaving them with the feeling that they have just had their soul raped? Worse still have you ever tried to justify yourself by slapping a 'noble cause label' on it? Did you think that would add weight to the mission of making them buckle and give in? Did that make you feel better about what we're doing to them? Did you throw a wobbly and have an emotional tantrum, when you couldn't make them do what you wanted?

As we ask ourselves these soul searching questions no one can help us with the answers except of course God himself! If we know we are guilty of these methods of operation, and sense God dealing with us accordingly, we need to co-operate with him. We need to repent and seek his forgiveness (for allowing spirits that are not of him to operate through us causing us to be unloving and therefore the opposite of all that he is). God is love and in those moments when we resort to these ungodly tactics, we are anything but that! We also need to seek to make it right with those whom we have hurt. If we are to be like

God we must come to understand and remember that he is a gentleman, not a rapist! He is all powerful and yet he never resorts to violation! As his people can we really justify behaving in a way that is opposite from everything he stands for?

The spirits of control and manipulation would hiss, spit, poison and slither, often slipping out into the dark of the night. They would then disappear into the bushes before anyone even realised what was going on. The venomous poison would literally get into the blood stream of the unfortunate person. Of course a powerful antidote was the only answer. If given in time the person and their whole life survived. Of course the challenge was always would the person and the antidote be united in time?

1 Corinthians chapter 2 verse 9/10/12
No eye has seen, no ear has heard, and no mind has imagined what God has prepared for those who love him. But we know these things because God has revealed them to us by his Spirit, and his Spirit, and his spirit searches out everything and shows us even God's deep secrets. And God has actually given us his spirit so we can know the wonderful things God has freely given us.

The revelation God gives us is life changing. It can actually be the difference between life and death! If God does not shed light on every aspect of our lives we will truly walk in darkness!

Daniel Chapter 9 verse 3, 21-23
So I turned to the Lord God and pleaded with him in prayer and fasting. I wore rough sackcloth and sprinkled myself with ashes.

As I was praying, Gabriel, whom I had seen in the earlier vision, came swiftly to me at the time at the evening sacrifice. He explained to me, Daniel, I have come here to give you insight and understanding. The moment you began praying, a command was given. I am here to tell you what it was, for God loves you very much. Now listen, so you can understand the meaning of your vision.

Daniel had been very disturbed by the visions that he'd received but didn't understand. He obviously knew they meant something but had absolutely no idea what. His confusion drove him to pray because he knew that only God could help him. He spoke to God determined to get the answer he needed. The answer came in no uncertain terms in the form of a visit from the angel Gabriel. He came complete with an explanation of the troubling vision, as well as an amazing and unique special reassurance that he was loved so much by God thrown in for good measure! What an awesome example of getting more than you bargain for.

John Chapter 8 verse 12
Jesus said to the people, "I am the light of the world. If you follow me, you won't be stumbling through the darkness, because you will have the light that leads to life."

When you love God enough to walk with him, and you know he loves you too, there is absolutely no good reason why you need to walk around in darkness when it comes to the things that really matter to you!

Through intense prayer God showed me things that I could never have known or find out without his revelation.

As I consider my life now I remain so grateful and indebted to God, for not abandoning me but instead giving me freedom. He showed me exactly what was going on. I was in shock that before prayer I couldn't see any of it. I take comfort from the scripture below:

John chapter 8 verse 32
You will know the truth and the truth and the truth will set you free.

Knowing the truth means knowing Jesus (who is the truth). Knowing Jesus means knowing yourself because he will show you the truth about you. This is the only thing that will bring true freedom. I believe this is why God desires for there to be truth (honesty) in our innermost being (heart) where it really counts! It doesn't matter how awful that truth may be, if we acknowledge it rather than live in denial and pretence, then God can and will help us to change for the better.

So in answer to prayer the Lord showed me the slithering snake and its relationship to Brenda. He showed me how as a result, it had access to slither in and out of my life because of my association with her. What he showed me through a dream was the straw that broke the camel's back. In the dream, Nigel and I were in bed. Brenda came into our bedroom looked at us with an unimpressed look on her face. Then suddenly as bold as brass she actually climbed into our bed with us! At that point Nigel put himself in the middle, so that he was between her and me. That way she could no longer interfere in our intimate time, and influence me.

This again was most disturbing! God showed me that although it certainly had her form and looked like Brenda, this was in fact the slithering snake and therefore the manifestation of a spirit. This spirit had the arrogance and audacity to defile our marriage bed (which is supposed to be sacred, private and intimate just between husband and wife)! It had managed to gain access due to my lack of prayer regarding Brenda. I had failed to set up adequate protective boundaries around my marriage. Therefore it felt it had the right to join us even in bed, and happily play absolute havoc with our home life.

This wasn't rocket science! I didn't suddenly need to become a genius to work out that I needed to get this spirit out of our bed and marriage! It was obvious that I needed to go cold turkey and break off my relationship with Brenda. It wasn't something I took lightly and it was such a bitter sweet thing to be honest. You don't love someone for a long time and suddenly turn a light switch off, and you're able to just stop over night. However I was at a cross road. The power of prayer and the perspective I had received from heaven, meant that obviously change was the only answer. After all my whole life was at stake here! It was different when I didn't have a clue. Now that God had shown me and I knew the truth, there was only one choice I could make. Still in spite of everything this was a huge struggle for me. So again I went to God. By now I had developed the praying bug, and decided it was wise to pray about everything including this.

"Lord just tell me one thing. I know the answer you give me will help me to let go of Brenda. Lord I really did love her with all my heart, and you know she was like a sister to me. Did she love me too? Did she ever really love me? What we shared was any of it even real? I just need to know."

Again the Lord soothed my broken heart. (This was becoming quite a habit)!

"Child of my love, it wasn't love. None of it was love. As you were naïve and trusting she found a way to use you. You had become a support pillar to hold up and build her life. Its in pretty much the same that a support pillar holds up a house," he answered gently.

His answer cut like a knife. However at this point I knew it was true and things started to fall into place. Suddenly I could see things more clearly than I had managed to previously. As I looked back forcing myself to be honest, I could see that all along I had always had my suspicions. However I had never wanted to believe badly of Brenda, so I ignored all the signs. My lack of prayer over this relationship made it so easy for things to happen as they did! An expensive lesson learned I might add. I include this story to warn of the dangers of taking things at face value, and seeing things as though through a dense fog. Prayer clears the fog and sheds precious light on what may have previously been hidden.

I was completely traumatised by the whole experience. How could this happen to me? How could I ensure it never happened again? How could I ever trust anyone ever again? How would I know who to trust in the future? I wondered.

Matthew Chapter 7 verses 15-27
Beware of false prophets who come disguised as harmless sheep, but are really wolves that will tear you apart. You can detect them by the way they act, just as you can identify a tree by its fruit. You don't pick grapes from thorn bushes, or figs from thistles. A healthy tree produces good fruit, and an unhealthy tree produces bad fruit. A good tree can't produce

bad fruit, and a bad tree can't produce good fruit. So every tree that does not produce good fruit is chopped down and thrown into the fire. Yes the way to identify a tree or a person is by the kind of fruit that is produced.

Not all people who sound religious are really godly. They may refer to me as Lord, but they still won't enter the kingdom of heaven. The decisive issue is whether they obey my father in heaven. On judgment day many will tell me, Lord, Lord we prophesied in your name and cast out demons in your name. But I will reply, I never knew you. Go away, the things you did were unauthorised.

Anyone who listens to my teaching and obeys me is wise, like a person who builds a house on solid rock. Though the rain comes in torrents and the flood waters rise and the winds beat against that house, it won't collapse because it is built on the rock. But anyone who hears my teaching and ignores it is foolish like a person who builds a house on sand. When the rain and floods come and the winds beat against that house, it will fall with a mighty crash.

The word of God if given a chance has an incredibly sobering effect. Considering it is jam packed full of God's mighty power how can we expect any less from it? It was good and powerful enough for God to use to create the heavens and the earth in the beginning. In the same way in this day and age it is just as potent and powerful.

As a result I have since learned that I have no option but to weigh up and measure everything up against the word of God. It has now become the standard that governs my life. It's the only way for it to remain protected and under the shadow of the Almighty! The other protective measure I adopted was to then bathe it fully in prayer! Now it really doesn't matter what people say or who they claim to be! From the above scripture the Lord taught me that life doesn't need to be confusing. If I really want to know the truth about someone, all I need to do is prayerfully look at the fruit of their lives. The fruit won't lie to me, in the same way that an apple tree will not be able to produce oranges! I decided there and then that I would eliminate fake people, their promises and every other form of imitation. There is now no longer any room for any of that! Every unhealthy soul tie has been broken, and through prayer I have applied the blood of Jesus. This has successfully closed up any gaps through which the enemy of my soul was previously able to crawl through! I have slammed the door in his face and on anything instigated by him!

Prayer has given me a brand new perspective and I will no longer settle for less than God's best for me. Why should I, when God assures and promises that I can have the real thing!

John chapter 16 verse 13-14

When the Spirit of truth comes, he will guide you into all truth. He will not be presenting his own ideas, he will be telling you what he has heard. He will tell you about the future. He will bring me glory by revealing to you whatever he receives from me.

With God's help I finally figured out what was holding me back. With his strength I let go and now by his grace I'm prayerfully moving on with my life. As difficult as it has been, I have come to understand something profound. It is far better to know the truth, and to face and deal with it accordingly.

James chapter 4 verse 7-8
So humble yourselves before God. Resist the Devil, and he will flee from you. Draw close to God, and God will draw close to you.

The above scripture sums up the key to a great and awesome life in God. Thankfully I can honestly say I have learned the most about my God when times have been the toughest. His awesome love for me has given me the heart of a giant. That heart now gives me what I need to be able to pray for others. As a result my prayer is that Jesus will find a special way to show you that he loves you too!

CHAPTER TEN

WHEN GOD'S MEN PRAYED

The bible is full of rich stories and accounts of the lives of men of God who prayed. It documents clearly the effect that prayer had on them. Once they adopted prayer as an essential part of who they were, their lives were never the same again. God himself acknowledges them as their stories unfold. What is revealed is the profound effect upon each life that enjoyed and experienced a deep and intimate relationship with the Almighty God.

Here is a list of some of the men of God who prayed and whose lives subsequently made a huge difference to those around them:

MOSES

Exodus chapter 17 verse 4
So Moses cried to the Lord, what shall I do with this people? They are almost ready to stone me.

Numbers chapter 12 verse 6-8
And the Lord said to them, Now listen to me! Even with prophets, I the Lord communicate by visions and dreams. But that is not how I communicate with my servant Moses. He is entrusted with my entire house. I speak to him face to face, directly and not in riddles!

Moses was a man of prayer who knew that unless he prayed, he would not be able to lead the people of Israel anywhere! The people were always complaining about one thing or another. If it was not about the lack of water or food, it was out of fear as their enemies pursued them. At times Moses found himself at the end of his tether because the people were ready to do him an injury. However he found his strength in knowing where to find God. He knew how to bring his questions to God and get the answers he needed. He developed a habit of having emergency meetings with God to find out what on earth he should do, regarding the many challenges he faced. His prayer life enabled him to live at a place where God could always speak to him. He always received instructions from heaven regarding the way he should proceed forward. God and Moses had such a close relationship, that God himself testified of what they shared! May God help us. May his grace work in us to develop the desire to be prepared to do whatever it takes to have an intimacy with him second to none!

JABEZ

1 Chronicles chapter 4 verse 10 – 11
Jabez was honourable above his brothers, but his mother named him Jabez (sorrow maker), saying, because I bore him in pain.

Jabez cried to the God of Israel, saying, Oh, that you would bless me and enlarge my border, and that your hand might be with me, and you would keep me from evil so it might not hurt me! And God granted his request.

Jabez must have started life with such an inferior complex, as his name meant (sorrow maker). This was because of the pain his mother experienced during childbirth. It seemed as if life itself was trying to defeat him from the very beginning. However thank God his story did not end here. Thank God he had the sense to pray!

Jabez was a man whose prayer changed his whole life. He prayed that God would bless him and give him all that he needed. He prayed that God would be with him so he was always protected from all manner of evil and would remain safe. The climax of the scripture is when we are informed of the conclusion; the God of heaven responded to his faith and actually granted his request! God just loves it when we believe in him, trust and look to him as our most vital option in life.

SOLOMON

1 Kings chapter 3 verse 3,5,9-13
Solomon loved the Lord and followed the instructions of his father, David except that Solomon too offered sacrifices and burned incense at the local altars.

That night The Lord appeared to Solomon in a dream, and God said, "What do you want? Ask, And I will give it to you!"

" Give me an understanding mind so that I can govern your people well and know the difference between right and wrong. For who by himself is able to govern this great nation of yours?" The Lord was pleased with Solomon's reply and was glad that he had asked for wisdom. So God replied, "Because you have asked for wisdom in governing my people, and have not asked for a long life or riches for yourself or the death of your enemies, I will give you what you asked for! I will give you a wise and understanding mind such as no one else has ever had or will ever have! And I will also give you what you did not ask for.. riches and honour! No other king in the entire world will be compared to you for the rest of your life!

In verse 3 we see that Solomon had a relationship with the Lord and loved him. So by verse 5, there was some serious communicating going on between them, based on the loving relationship they shared. The Lord decided to ask Solomon what he wanted from him as a gift, as he was ready to bless him.

Solomon found himself in the unfamiliar position of being the new king. He was following in the steps of his father the great king David, of whom God had said, 'a man after my own heart'. It was not easy for him to fill his father's shoes, as he felt completely out of his depth. He was under more than just a little pressure! He was totally intimidated by the daunting weight of the great task ahead of him. His inexperience taunted him and his feelings of inadequacy seemed greatly magnified. He wondered if he was even up to the job. His prayer was a heartfelt cry to the God he knew could help him. He asked for wisdom, understanding, and a hearing heart. He knew he needed help to be sensitive to God's Spirit. He knew he would have to depend on him to lead, guide and direct him every step of the way. He acknowledged honestly and vulnerably that without God's help he didn't stand a chance. In himself alone he was not equipped to do the job. As it happens his request thrilled and pleased God so much. God's granted his request and gave him everything he did not even ask for on top, as good measure!

ELIJAH

1 kings chapter 18 verses 36-39

At the customary time for offering the evening sacrifice, Elijah the prophet walked up to the altar and prayed, "O Lord God of Abraham, Isaac and Jacob, prove today that you are God in Israel and that I am your servant. Prove that I have done all this at your command. O Lord answer me! Answer me so that these people will know that you, O Lord, are God and that you have brought them back to yourself."

Immediately the fire of the Lord flashed down from heaven and burned up the young bull, the wood, the stones, and the dust. It even licked up all the water in the ditch! And when the people saw it, they fell on their faces and cried out, "The Lord is God! The Lord is God!"

Elijah prayed expecting his prayer to be answered. His confidence was based on the fact that (a) he belonged to God (b) his intention was to glorify God (c) he had been obedient and done all that God had told him to. Elijah met all the necessary requirements for his prayer to be effective and therefore answered by the living God who answered unmistakably by fire. By the end of the incident, there was no doubt that God was happy to turn up and do what only he could, confirming the word of his servant.

JACOB

Genesis Chapter 32 verse 24-30

This left Jacob all alone in the camp, and a man came and wrestled with him until dawn. When the man saw that he couldn't win the match, he struck Jacob's hip and knocked it out joint at the socket. Then the man said, "let me go, for it is dawn. But Jacob panted, "I will not let you go unless you bless me." "What is your name?" the man asked.

He replied Jacob. "Your name will no longer be Jacob," the man told him." It is now Israel, because you have struggled with both God and men and have won."

But Jacob stayed behind by himself, and a man wrestled with him until daybreak. When the man saw that he couldn't get the best of Jacob as they wrestled, he deliberately threw Jacob's hip out of joint.

The man said what's your name? He answered, Jacob. The man said, but no longer. Your name is no longer Jacob. From now on its Israel (God wrestler); You've wrestled with God and you've come through. Jacob asked and what's your name? And then, right then and there he blessed him. Jacob named the place Peniel God's face because, he said, I saw God face to face and lived to tell the story.

Jacob's prayer was a wrestling one. It suggests great effort, exertion, persistence, resilience, and a determination to say that he was not about to give up without a fight. He fought in prayer to the point that he was physically injured during the process! He would not let go until he got what he set out to receive from God. After his entire destiny was at stake. He must have discerned deep down inside in his spirit, that this was his once in a lifetime opportunity. He instinctively knew that it was literally now or never. He craved the experience of a dramatic change in his life. However up until this point it had always successfully evaded him. Jacob was tired of life as he knew it had really had enough! He was sick and tired of the promise that tomorrow would be a better day. His experience had been that it never was! When he met God he was on a focused mission. After wrestling with

God, the Lord was so impressed with him, that he not only received his blessing but a brand new respectable name also. Jacob believed that he had seen God face to face and this changed his life forever! The awesome amazing truth is that if you want to meet God in this way, your life will never be the same either! Go on I dare you! Why don't you start all over again and introduce yourself?

JOSHUA

Joshua Chapter 10 verses 12-14
Then Joshua spoke to the Lord on the day when the Lord gave the Amorites over to the Israelites, and he said in the sight of Israel, sun be silent and stand still at Gibeon, and you moon, in the valley of Ajalon! And the sun stood still and the moon stayed, until the nation took vengeance upon their enemies. Is not this written in the book of Jasher? So the sun stood still in the midst of the heavens and did not hasten to go down for about a whole day. There was no day like it before or since, when the Lord heeded the voice of a man. For the Lord fought for Israel.

Joshua and his people were at war with their enemies and the Lord had been a great help to his people enabling them to be experience victory. After Joshua conversed with the Lord he found himself so full of faith. This faith gave him the confidence to be able to literally speak to and command the sun and moon to stand still. He was able to affect the natural order of things, by exercising his God given dominion. This was a great advantage for God's people as there was daylight all day long. They could just get on with doing a great job defeating their enemies. It was truly a day like no other as the Lord God listened to Joshua and fought for his people.

DANIEL

Daniel Chapter 9 verses 3, 21-23
And I set my face to the Lord God to seek him by prayer and supplications, with fasting and sackcloth and ashes.

Yes, while I was speaking in prayer, the man Gabriel whom I had seen in the former vision, being caused to fly swiftly, came near to me and touched me about the time of the evening sacrifice. He instructed me and made me understand; he talked with me and said, oh Daniel, I am now come forth to give you skill and wisdom and understanding. At the beginning of your prayers, the word giving an answer went forth, and I have come to tell you, for you are greatly beloved. Therefore consider the matter and understand the vision.

Daniel was focused and determined to prayerfully talk things over with the Lord and even fast as there was great need. As a result of his prayer an angel was sent to minister and comfort him. He was informed that in response to his prayers a word from heaven had been sent to bring him answers. He was also told that he was greatly loved by God.

Daniel chapter 10 verse 12-14
Relax Daniel, he continued, don't be afraid. From the moment you decided to humble yourself to receive understanding, your prayer was heard, and I set out to come to you. But I was waylaid by the angel prince of the kingdom of Persia and was

delayed for a good three weeks. But then Michael, one of the chief angel princes intervened to help me.

The angel reassured him and explained that the very first day Daniel had prayed, his prayer had been heard in heaven and this very angel had been sent as a result. There was however unfortunately a delay. The angel found himself in deep spiritual warfare encountering obstacles that hindered things in the heavenlies. (Spiritual hemisphere) It took assistance from other heavenly warriors before the angel could proceed with his mission. However in spite of the challenges, what was rightfully Daniel's from heaven could not be stopped or interfered with indefinitely.

JESUS

Luke chapter 6 verse 12-13
At about the same time he climbed a mountain to pray. He was there all night in prayer before God. The next day he summoned his disciples. From them he selected twelve he designated as apostles.

Interestingly Jesus had spent the whole night in prayer to his father. Jesus had huge decisions to make and he couldn't afford to get it wrong. There was just too much was at stake. After his night in prayer he was fully equipped with the wisdom to choose the right people. These people would be closest to him and carry on his work and mission when the time came.

Luke chapter 9 verses 16-17
He took the five loaves and two fish, lifted his face to heaven in prayer, blessed, broke, and gave the bread and fish to his disciples to hand out to the crowd. After the people had all eaten their fill, twelve baskets of leftovers were gathered up.

Jesus did an awesome miracle by taking next to nothing and making a feast for many, with food left over. He literally did the impossible and was able to do so out of what he shared with his father. He proved that a strong relationship with God born out of a healthy prayer life, can and does lead to a life full of miracles. Prayer is always the source that can provide help for whatever is the pressing need.

John chapter 11 verses 41-44
They removed the stone. Jesus raised his eyes to heaven and prayed, "father I'm grateful that you have listened to me. I know that you always do listen, but on account of this crowd standing here I've spoken so that they might believe that you sent me. Then he shouted "Lazarus come out! And he came out, wrapped from head to toe, and with a kerchief over his face. Jesus told them, "Unwrap him and let him loose."

This scene was one of the finest hours of Jesus' Life. It spoke volumes about who he is. The tension in the air must have been electrifying. The expectancy, grief, disbelief, scepticism as well as his own emotional involvement could have put Jesus under serious pressure. In fact it could have completely put him off meeting the demands of the task. However, he approached the challenge in the way that was characteristic of the way he lived his life. Jesus always looked up to discern Heaven's

KNOCKING ON HEAVEN'S DOOR

verdict first. Once he was sure, his actions then reflected and mirrored on earth whatever was heaven's take on things. In spite of his humanity he never forgot, or allowed himself to get caught up in the moment. He never forgot his mission because his focus remained ever before him. His prayer life was the engine that enabled him to affect critics and fans alike, changing the very fabric of history itself.

John chapter 17 verse 9,13-15
I'm not praying for the God rejecting world, but for those you gave me, for they are yours by right. Now I'm returning to you. I'm saying these things in the world's hearing so my people can experience my joy completed in them. I gave them your word; The godless world hated them because of it, because they didn't join the world's ways. I'm not asking that you take them out of the world, but that you guide them from the evil one.

Jesus prayed for us even before we were born, just because we are his people whom he greatly loves. What amazing comfort it brings to know that he was thinking of us even then. His prayers for us were paving the way and making the path clear for us well in advance!

Luke chapter 22 verses 39-44
Leaving there, he went, as he so often did, to mount olives. The disciples followed him. When they arrived at the place, he said, pray that you don't give into temptation. He pulled away from them about a stone's throw, knelt down and prayed, "Father remove this cup from me. But please, not what I want. What do you want? At once an angel from heaven was at his side, strengthening him. He prayed on all the harder. Sweat, wrung from him like drops of blood, poured off his face.

It was a habit of Jesus to go off periodically to pray. The son of God himself needed to cultivate such a lifestyle and keep his lifeline to heaven open. The life he lived presented challenges at every turn. He had to constantly fall back on his prayer life and his God. This obviously empowered and equipped him to continue to be the man he was, even to the end. The most intense and ultimate pressure was upon him. The whole point of his mission was always before him, but when it came to the crunch, Jesus felt overwhelmed. He struggled deeply with what was required of him. He came face to face with the reality and the implications of what he was about to do. There was no turning back and he found it almost too much to bear. The more he thought about it, the more he wondered if perhaps this was not such a good idea. He prayed that maybe there would be some other way. The pressure he felt was so intense that it showed physically. As blood vessels began to burst what started off as drops of sweat became drops of blood. Thankfully the more stressed he became, the more he had the presence of mind to intensify his prayers. This truly was an emergency. He had come this far and couldn't bring himself to give up, even though he felt like there was too much resting on his shoulders. If he failed and the mission had to be aborted, the way he had spoken and lived his life up until this point, would have been in vain. The father's plan to offer mankind hope would have been frustrated.

Jesus channelled everything he felt into praying like never before, until it was established forever what he must do. He prayed until he received the peace and ability to do what he could only do with heaven's help. When he received that breakthrough in the spirit realm, only then did he return to his disciples and wake them up. Finally the time for his betrayal had come. Finally it was time to fulfil God's plan to save humanity!

CHAPTER ELEVEN

PRAYER RECORDING

Habakkuk chapter 2 verse 1-3

I will climb up into my watchtower now and wait to see what the Lord will say to me and how he will answer my complaint. Then the Lord said to me, "write my answer in large, clear letters on a tablet, so that a runner can read it, and tell everyone else. But these things I plan won't happen right away. Slowly, steadily, surely, the time approaches when the vision will be fulfilled. If it seems slow, wait patiently, for it will surely take place. It will not be delayed.

It was God's idea to record our prayer journey. He knew that doing so would help us to stay focused. It would also help us to stay encouraged as we fight and strive to keep our vision alive. How better to be able to work with him, enabling his plan to be fulfilled in our lives?

I have always found it a good idea to keep accurate records of my prayer life. Prayer is such a remarkable adventure. There are so many areas that need prayer cover. As we serve a prayer answering God, at the right time the answers will definitely come. It is therefore always a blessing to note what the request was, the result and answer. It is worth noting exactly what took place. It is also good to know the length of time it took for the answer to come. Obviously depending on what the request is the window of time may vary. Some answers will seem to come quickly, while others will seem as if God forgot to look at his watch! The point is God's timing and ours are completely different. We should bear in mind that he sees the whole picture while we only see in part. Therefore it is worth waiting for him to do what we cannot. We should also record the difference that prayer made, for future reference. It is also helpful to document proof of the power of prayer, as this is a great source of encouragement to us as well as to others.

SECTION ONE:

PRAYER JOURNALS

I have always found that keeping a prayer journal helps me log my personal walk with the Lord. I often log my prayers, battles, struggles, victories, and conversations with the Lord. I find I am greatly strengthened as I look back and note personal spiritual growth. The bible invites us to come boldly before God's throne. We do so in order to receive the grace and mercy from God that we need to help us in our time of need. By keeping a prayer journal I have been able to document practical and intimate details, of how I applied certain bible verses to each and every situation that arose. I have been able to look back and be encouraged. Learning from my mistakes hopefully I can urge and inspire others to do things differently.

Keeping a prayer journal provides the opportunity to be able to reflect on things and meditate on the Lord's answers to each scenario that arises. In my prayer journals I have recorded practical aspects of my journey with Jesus. There have been so many precious things that have happened. I want them etched in history and my memory forever. It is some of these things that I have shared with you in previous chapters.

So recording things accurately helps ensure this is so much more than just wishful thinking. Of course a perfect example are those awesome times when my beloved, my first and last, my knight in shining armour, the lover of my soul, Jesus, has revealed himself to me in ways too precious for words. My prayer journal has attempted to record such moments forever. Keeping a prayer journal has enriched my life and affected my personal growth profoundly. One of the reasons is because it helps me stay prayerfully focused on me. It is essential that I do everything I can to ensure I am keeping myself right before the Lord. This has got to become the basis for who I am, and everything I do! I am encouraged to grow in character and aim to be like my God. This certainly beats blaming everyone else including my upbringing, the government, and other people for every wrong thing in my life. I've found you don't grow very much by blaming others for everything! Having a prayer journal forces the issue. It removes the option of choosing not to take personal responsibility for my life, and how I choose to live it!

A prayer journal is a very individual and personal thing so there is no right or wrong way of keeping one. Nothing has to be set in stone. As a person grows the way they record their personal journey with Jesus, will evolve accordingly. However for some ideas, and helpful tips, you may like to record your favourite prayers, psalms, and praise and thanksgiving moments. On the other hand when going through the most challenging, deepest valley of your walk with God, it might be helpful to record the most vivid expressions of God's love for you. Don't forget to mention all the ways that he tenderly reminds you of his presence. It might also help to record the prayers where all you could manage was a heart wrenching cry for help.

Sometimes things will not go too well as this is just part of life. If you have needed to repent and (have a change of heart about things), it is worth recording it as a landmark to say from this day onwards things will be different. The peaks and the valleys are what make your own personal walk so colourful and your journey so special. Your own journey will always be worth recording as there will never be another quite like it! Keeping a prayer journal will serve as a constant reminder that your prayer life will reflect the very core of who you are. Both of these things are therefore worth celebrating very much.

SECTION TWO

PRAYER REQUEST FORMS AND PRAYER BOXES

A simple prayer request form to record information accurately can be implemented as follows:

PERSON'S NAME:

DATE OF PRAYER REQUEST :

DESCRIPTION OF PRAYER NEED:

HEALING (PHYSICAL, EMOTIONAL, MENTAL)

(Tick as appropriate)

SALVATION

DELIVERANCE

FINANCIAL

ANY OTHER HELP NEEDED FROM THE LORD

PRAYER REQUEST:

RELEVANT SCRIPTURE PROMISE:

PRAYER ANSWER AND TESTIMONY:

As my prayer life developed and I learned how to pray about everything, I found that I had dozens of prayer request forms everywhere. I decided it would be better to get organised and have all the requests in one place instead. Therefore I started keeping them all in a special box. At intervals I would pray over the box again and again. Sometimes reminding the Lord, other times thanking and praising him for the results that would be seen in the natural world. This is my way of bringing the requests before the Lord, knowing that I can leave them with him because he is totally trustworthy. I know that even before I pray, he has prepared and tailor made an answer just for me. I know it is his aim to meet my prayer requests and the needs I lay before him. It also helps me know that I have not just seen a need and thought, "oh what a shame," but I have actually done something useful about it.

CHAPTER TWELVE

PRAYER MEETINGS

(A GATHERING OF GOD'S PRAYER WARRIORS)

Revelation chapter 5 verse 8
The moment he took the scroll, the four animals and twenty four elders fell down and worshipped the lamb. Each had a harp and each had a bowl, a gold bowl filled with incense, the prayers of God's people.

Revelation chapter 8 verse 3-5
Then another angel with a gold incense burner came and stood at the altar. And a great quantity of incense was given to him to mix with the prayers of God's people, to be offered on the gold altar before the throne. The smoke of the incense, mixed with the prayers of the saints, ascended up to God form the altar where the angel had poured them out. Then the angel filled the incense burner with fire from the altar and threw it down upon the earth, and thunder crashed, lightening flashed, and there was a terrible earthquake.

Picture the scene if you will. Everyone before the throne fell down before the lamb of God and worshipped him. They couldn't help it. They worshipped him because they all knew he deserved it. Each one held a golden bowl full to the brim of special incense. This incense was made up of the precious prayers of all God's people all over the world.

We can be comforted when we read the above scriptures that explain exactly what happen to our prayers. In spite of how we may feel at times, our prayers do not just bounce off the walls, having no effect! Instead, they are literally transported to heaven on a mission, and their final destination is the very throne of God, where Jesus the lamb is worshipped. There is no better place for our prayers to end up because here they receive God's undivided attention! Heaven itself then sends a response to our prayer, to deal with whatever the challenge is and meet the need on earth.

Now please picture the second scene. A particular angel has the task of standing at the altar with a golden incense burner. His job is to mix the large quantity of incense he has been given, with the prayers of God's people. He then has to offer it on the altar before God's throne, allowing the smoke to rise into God's presence. After a time the angel refills the incense burner with fire from the same altar, and throws that down on to the earth, affecting and changing it forever!

A prayer meeting therefore is a gathering of God's people who have come together for the express purpose of praying together, as opposed to individually. It is based on the understanding that there is great spiritual power made available during this time. It certainly is not about the quantity of people present. Rather it is all about the fact that Jesus is in the midst of his people. His great power therefore is released and in full operation. When we come together in unity he promised that it would be! The purpose of getting together therefore is to utilise that power as a unified front. The aim is to effect change in the Spiritual realm and subsequently the natural realm, and therefore in our world as we know it. We want to be able to say to God Almighty in effect, 'Let your kingdom be established on earth as it is already established in heaven.'

Whenever God's people are unified in purpose, mission, words and action, it is an opportunity to declare that Jesus will build his church on this earth! It also confirms that the gates of hell shall not be able to prevail against it. Praying together therefore ensures that the terms of this covenant agreement with God, are carried out enforcing his perfect will on this earth.

There are different types of prayer meetings. There are general meetings where just about every type of prayer need is prayed for. There are also the more specific type of prayer meeting where the prayer content is more focused and concentrated on particular areas of need. It is in these sorts of meetings where prayer covering is provided for particular people, ministries, churches, or challenges.

To give examples, many years ago there were two different prayer meetings that I attended on a regular basis. The first one was monthly and usually took place on a Friday night. It took place at the church that I attended. It was made up of people from different nations, who all love Jesus. It was a place where lives truly were being transformed daily by the power of God. Its primary focus was reaching out, touching and making a difference to the people around and the community at large.

At one meeting we received a prayer request concerning a young mother who had just given birth to twins. Subsequently she developed a heart problem, and was too poorly to go home, let alone take care of her babies. At the prayer meeting we prayed for her, declaring God's word over her and applying the blood of Jesus over her and every aspect of her health. A few weeks later during a subsequent prayer meeting, we received a report that this same lady was now on the mend and well enough to go home with her babies!

At another Friday night prayer meeting, the Pastor felt the need to pray for the single people of the church. We therefore prayed that there would be such a move of God that each one would find their lifelong partner, and no longer have to continue on in loneliness any longer. By the Sunday of that same week, during the morning service, a couple announced that they had found each other and planned to spend the rest of their lives together! In the evening service of that same day, a young man went to the front of the church and asked his girlfriend to stand and then join him at the front. When she did, he proposed to her there and then right in the middle of the service in front of everyone. Thankfully she said yes once she got over her shock! Every person that had been at the previous Friday night prayer meeting, was nearly besides themselves with excitement at the goodness of God. Part of the excitement was having the privilege of being a co worker with God and having a small part to play in the great things happening in response to the prayers of God's people!

The other prayer meeting I attended took place once a fortnight. This functioned as the engine room and the heart of the church. This prayer meeting was more specific in nature, as it covered all aspects of all that was happening at the church. This prayer was intercessory in nature, so we prayed for the church leaders, (The members of the Pastoral team) as well as for the church members. We prayed about each challenge that arose. We also prayed for revelation as well as for God's perfect will to be done in every church department. As the Lord (by the Holy Spirit) revealed what he desired concerning his church, we actively and determinedly prayed it through. We continued until we felt the release in the 'spirit realm' that it was done. As a result of prayer there have been healings and many broken people have been restored. We prayed passionately for them until we saw the power of God meet them at the point of their need, changing their lives forever. It is always incredibly exciting to receive reports of answered prayer and testimonies, about what God is doing all over the world as his people take up the challenge to pray!

CHAPTER THIRTEEN

A CLOSING THOUGHT

We are all invited to knock on heaven's door at any time.

Whether or not the door is opened in answer to our specific knock, depends largely on our relationship with the King of Kings! He is after all the king of heaven and there is no higher power or authority. The buck stops with him.

In all honesty I'm sure you will agree, it is not exactly easy to get through this maze of a thing called life. Therefore the person who believes they can manage without having the Lord on their side, or a map for the journey, (because they place little or no value in his word), proves that they are not the wisest of people. In view of the challenges that life often presents, truthfully such people are defeated before they have even begun. If only they knew this, maybe many of their choices would be a lot different!

Unfortunately there is an unseen enemy out there ready to destroy them. Without the mighty weapon of prayer to combat his assaults, they will most likely be tossed about by which ever wind he chooses to blow into their lives at any given time.

The great news is that we all have the gift of choice, and it doesn't need to be this way. We can choose to be a mighty victorious force to be reckoned with in the spirit realm! This is God's plan for us. However whether or not the plan is fulfilled, depends on if we follow Moses example. On God's instruction he stopped panicking long enough to change his mindset, step out in faith and use what he had in his hand! He was not disappointed in the end because he got to see God's faithfulness in action. The point is that if we do the same, we will also experience the same blessings.

1 Corinthians chapter 1 verses 8-9
He will keep you strong right up to the end, and he will keep you free from all blame on the great day when our Lord Jesus Christ returns. God will surely do this for you, for he always does just what he says, and he is the one who invited you into this wonderful friendship with his son, Jesus Christ our Lord.

As we take the time to invest in the most important relationship we could ever have, (our relationship with God), he himself will establish us. He will establish our lives, weaving his own strength into its very core, foundation and roots. The result will turn out to be that we are immovable, fixed and stable in all we are and all we do. This will apply regardless of the circumstances we face, or the challenges we are forced to deal with.

A major part of God's character is that he is faithful. Those who put all their trust in him, and learn to depend on him completely find that they are never alone. Rather they are always able to enjoy the comfort of his presence, even in their most challenging moments! This is something you can never know unless you personalise it for yourself! You have to go on your own journey with God. You can't live off someone else's testimony or just by what they say! It won't work unless you take the risk to try it for yourself! When you find the courage to take the plunge then what you and God share should be the most intimate, passionate and beautiful thing in your life. Just the very thought of him should affect you more deeply than anything else! Just remember he went to the very end of the earth to die, just to prove his love for you. He then rose again to settle it in your heart forever. This love of your life is a love like no other!

Psalm 37 verses 23-24
The steps of the godly are directed by the Lord. He delights in every detail of their lives. Though they stumble, they will not fall, for the Lord holds them by the hand.

Those who belong to the Lord can live life knowing that they are blessed. There is no need for them to find themselves aimlessly and helplessly plodding along, just hoping for the best. Their lives are much too precious for that! After all destiny, meaning and purpose are waiting to take hold! The Lord himself gives direction and gets intimately involved in their every step. He has a plan and blue print for each of us, and the answer to every question our lives could possibly be challenged by. Even in the midst of the worst kind of trouble, we don't need to be defeated. The Lord himself grasps us and holds us close to him, supporting us all the way.

Malachi chapter 3 verse 10-12
Bring all the tithes into the store house so there will be enough food in my temple. If you do, says the Lord Almighty, I will open the windows of heaven for you. I will pour out a blessing so great you won't have enough room to take it in! Try it! Let me prove it to you! Your crops will be abundant, for I will guard them from insects and disease. Your grapes will not shrivel before they are ripe, says the Lord Almighty.

The Lord sets us a challenge as he invites us to bring our tithes to him. Our tithes do not just refer to our money, but actually means the very best of all we have and the very best of ourselves. It is not so much what we give. Rather it is so much more to do with the attitude that motivates us to give in the first place. This is what really matters and therefore what God is interested in. It is healthy practise to ask the Lord always to reveal to us the truth about our giving. Often our own hearts are contaminated and therefore have great capacity to deceive us. Only the Lord truly knows and sees all things clearly. So what matters to him the most are our hearts intentions. The truth is we cannot out give God! He therefore challenges us to test him in this, and prove this for ourselves. He promises to deal with any enemy seeking to make us believe that we are anything but blessed!

Malachi chapter 3 verse 13-15
You have said terrible things about me says the Lord.
But you say what do you mean? How have we spoken against you? You have said what's the use of serving God? What have we gained by obeying his commands or by trying to show the Lord Almighty that we are sorry for our sins? From now on we will say, blessed are the arrogant. For those who do evil get rich, and those who dare God to punish them go free of harm.

The Lord reveals that he is aware of all those people who speak harshly against him and his ways. These same people believe it is pointless to have a relationship with him, to serve him, and to strive to be right before him. They are offended because in their estimation, it seems that those who choose to be evil, seem to be having a party and a great time in life. Their reasoning seems to be, "what is the point? Why bother?" they ask.

Malachi chapter 3 verse 16-18
Then those who feared the Lord spoke with each other, and the Lord listened to what they said. In his presence, a scroll of remembrance was written to record the names of those who feared him and loved to think about him. They will be my people says the Lord Almighty. On the day when I act, they will be my own special treasure. I will spare them as a father spares an obedient and dutiful child. Then you will again see the difference between the righteous and the wicked, between those who serve God and those who do not.

The bottom line is that God knows those who are his. He listens to the conversations of his people, and makes notes about those who spend time thinking about him. He gladly receives such people. He makes a public declaration that they belong to and are so special to him. As a matter of fact, in life there appears to be such a clear distinction between those people who belong to him and are blessed by him, and those who choose to have nothing to do with him at all, and their lives are not.

1 Peter chapter 5 verses 6-10
So humble yourselves under the mighty power of God, and in his good time he will honour you. Give all your worries and cares to God, for he cares about what happens to you. Be careful! Watch out for attacks from the Devil, your great enemy. He prowls around like a roaring lion, looking for some victim to devour. Take a firm stand against him, and be strong in your faith. In his kindness God called you to his eternal glory by means of Jesus Christ. After you have suffered a little while ,

he will restore, support and strengthen you, and he will place you on a firm foundation.

We are given clear instructions by God the one who knows all things. When we diligently follow what he says, we will find his wisdom helpful. Our lives then are much more likely to become a success story. They also become a channel through which the power of God can move, providing the answers needed for others through prayer.

Humility is such a valuable quality to be developed. Seeing ourselves as we really are, vulnerable and not immune to any of life's storms, is the reality of every human being. It is therefore a good idea to embrace this truth. We must make a conscious effort to develop a balanced view of our own importance. This will help to remind us of our complete dependence on God. Almighty God who then searches our hearts and knows us better than we even knows ourselves, is then free to promote us in the right way and at the right time.

We are reminded that God cares so much about us and watches over us. It is therefore so right and good for us to bring everything to him, including whatever is a worry, concern, or cause for anxiety. Jesus is our hero and champion ready to sort it all out for us!

If we stick close to him and cover everything in prayer, we are more equipped and likely to be balanced as people. We will also be more aware of the attacks of the devil as he continues to prove that he is indeed the enemy of our souls. The truth is that he is always looking for an opportunity to trip us up, and harm us in any way he can. An intimate relationship with God and a prayerful lifestyle keeps Satan where he belongs, under our feet! Only then will we be well equipped to stand up to him.

Only then will we be confident enough to remind him that Jesus our commander in chief, has already defeated and shamed him! As the battle of life rages we may suffer (because we live in a fallen world). However the plan is for Satan to come off worse because our God has already dealt with him! Jesus has already done all that is necessary to establish us in strength, and to fill our lives with a sure certainty that we are blessed.

Job chapter 22 verse 21-30
Stop quarrelling with God! If you agree with him, you will have peace at last, and things will go well for you. Listen to his instructions, and store them in your heart. If you return to the Almighty and clean up your life, you will be restored. Give up your lust for money, and throw your precious gold into the river. Then the Almighty himself will be your treasure. He will be your precious silver! Then you will delight yourself in the Almighty and look up to God. You will pray to him, and he will hear you, and you will fulfil your vows to him. Whatever you decide to do will be accomplished, and light will shine on the road ahead of you. If someone is brought low and you say, help him up, God will save the downcast. Then even sinners will be rescued by your pure hands.

We are encouraged to get to know God, and to line our lives up with the standard of his will for our lives. We need to get used to his way of doing things, because he knows best. This will bring us peace and fill our lives with prosperity, (all that is good and everything that we could possibly need). The best way forward is to spend time becoming familiar with his word, and all that it takes to be right with him.

If we take the time and put in the energy to make this our heart's passion, we will automatically find our faith will be strong. This is what happens when we are so in tune with him. Our faith becomes strong when we are built up inside, to the point where we will gladly exchange the things of this world for our relationship with God. We must learn to choose to put him high above all else. This is one of the hardest lessons ever. It therefore helps to practise the art of considering what we have with him. Then take that to the next level and know that it is the most precious and priceless thing in our possession. The conclusion will then inevitably be that awesome things will happen. In the Spirit realm we will be powerful and unstoppable! As God himself becomes our delight in life, then we will be able to stand boldly before him, lifting our faces up to him. When we pray he will hear and answer, making our lives not only significant but also meaningful.

Working in partnership we will jointly make decisions with him. Based on the authority of his word, we will be in the privileged position of being able to declare and decree certain things on this earth. When we pray and intercede for others, it will make a big difference and have great impact. As God's favour shines upon us, he will establish these things for us because heaven has already approved and joined us to say amen!

Psalm 84 verse 11
For the Lord God is our light and protector. He gives us grace and glory. No good thing will the Lord withhold from those who do what is right.

As God shields us from life's storms he promises not to with-hold anything good from those who are his.

Luke chapter 12 verse 31-32
He will give you all you need from day to day if you make the kingdom of God your primary concern. So don't be afraid, little flock. For it gives your father great happiness to give you the kingdom.

As we put God first he will give us all that we need, because it is actually his pleasure to give us all he has in his kingdom. Even more than that he will give us more than we need in an abundant fashion.

Psalm chapter 127 verses 1-2
Unless the Lord builds the house, the work of the builders is useless. Unless the Lord protects a city, guarding it with sentries will do no good. It is useless for you to work so hard from early morning until late at night, anxiously working for food to eat, for God gives rest to his loved ones.

We all have the inclination and ability to build. Our very lives can be compared to a house that has been built. However unless it is the Lord building the house, the building done is actually done in vain. Sooner or later the house will run into problems. Many do all that they think it takes to achieve, and get somewhere in life, only to find out that life itself seems to be against them! They feel the sting of failure and the pain of fighting a ruthless enemy they cannot even see. They become depressed, defeated, and suicidal and melancholy, wondering what life is all about anyway. The answers seem to cruelly evade them and laugh in the shadows.

In the meantime the people of God learn not to trust in their own limitations. Instead they allow God to build their lives in the way it was meant to be. As a result they enjoy a great measure of freedom. As an extra bonus they also enjoy the gift he gives of being able to sleep at night.

Matthew chapter 16 verses 15-19
Then he asked them, "Who do you say I am?" Simon Peter answered, "You are the Messiah, the Son of the living God." Jesus replied, "You are blessed, Simon son of John, because my father in heaven has revealed this to you. You did not learn this from any human being. Now I say to you that you are Peter, and upon this rock I will build my church, and all the powers of hell will not conquer it. And I will give you the keys to the kingdom of heaven. Whatever you lock on earth will be locked in heaven, and whatever you open on earth will be opened in heaven."

The Lord God Almighty challenges us with a searching question. We are to research, consider, ponder and come to a conclusion regarding who we believe God is in our lives. It doesn't matter who we are, we can never be exempt from answering the question. It is so vital and of such paramount importance that it will not go away. We may answer, we don't believe in him, he means nothing to us, we don't need him because we are just too busy doing it our way. On the other hand we may have received a revelation of who he is and how much we actually do need him. Jesus commended Peter on discovering this truth. He declared that based upon this revelation sent down from heaven, he as God was going to build his church. Once God's people really grasp who he is, this allows him to be able to build their lives in the way they were always intended to be. He then promises that not all the powers, attempts, or attacks of hell, would be able to ruin or have free rein to cause havoc or harm to such lives! In fact the opposite will be true as he actually gives us the keys to the kingdom of heaven. Not only will we be victorious in our own lives, but through prayer we will be equipped to enforce victory in the lives of others also. When this happens again and again all over the world, then it is inevitable that the church of God will grow from strength to strength. The people of God will be able to confidently declare 'Let your will be done on this earth even as it is done in heaven!' This will move from being a hopeful ideal to a reality that is being fulfilled each day.

Isaiah chapter 22 verse 22
I will give him the key to the house of David, the highest position in the royal court. He will open doors, and no-one will be able to shut them, he will close doors, and no one will be able to open them.

As we receive the keys from our commander in chief, and his very own authority to use on earth, we will be able to open or shut doors in the spirit realm according to his instructions. Through having a relationship with God and praying to him, nothing will be impossible for us to achieve through our lives, and on behalf of others.

The one who lives a life of prayer has the privilege of having a bird's eye view of life. The heavenly perspective ensures we are now able to see the bigger picture. It is vastly different from viewing life from the limited perspective of the natural realm, where the only choice we have is to just hope for the best.

Finally, it is encouraging to remember what an awesome blessing it is to be able to live life with a prayerful attitude. The whole point of knocking on heaven's door is to receive certain assurance that heaven has indeed agreed to invade earth! When it does, it brings with it all its glory, majesty and awesome splendour! Talk about spicing things up. The result is that the dull, drab, and mundane is transformed. There are glimpses of brilliant light in the same way that a shooting star lights up the darkest of skies.

A life of prayer is a life that imitates the one lived by Jesus our commander in chief. At present he lives in heaven and continuously prays and intercedes for his people. We can work in partnership with him by joining him in prayer, as he reveals the desperate needs of this world. It is an honour to work with him and to see things change, as they bow to the power of God made available through prayer. We are invited to be a part of this.

So I challenge you, next time you or someone you know finds themselves in a sticky situation, what will you do? Will you be the one who makes a difference setting the captive free, or will you just stand there feeling helpless and frustrated? Will you dare to look at what that is in your hand? Are you prepared to even go a step further? Will you perfect the art of taking the time to be still in each situation that presents itself? You need to know beyond the shadow of doubt, that he is not just God out there somewhere, far removed from the things that really matter to you, but that he is actually the God of your life. He loves you more than ever and is even closer to you than your next breath! Why don't you call him and see what happens? Why don't you pray and release the power that nothing can stop? You may not get what you expect but I guarantee you will never be the same again after the experience!

Matthew chapter 11 verse 28
Then Jesus said, come to me, all of you who are weary and carry heavy burdens, and I will give you rest. Take my yoke upon you. Let me teach you because I am humble and gentle, and you will find rest for your souls. For my yoke fits perfectly, and the burden I give you is light.

In conclusion let us receive great comfort from the above scripture and promise. Jesus tells us in a nutshell that he is fully committed to us and cares deeply about our wellbeing. The pressing question then is how are you going to respond? Are you going to rise to the challenge of knocking on heaven's door? After all you never know what might happen as a result!

ABOUT THE AUTHOR

Diane Wilkie is a freelance writer and author. She wrote 'The only arranged marriage,' the authorised biography of Raj Jarrett. She also co-authored 'Run for your life,' an exciting African mystery novel, full of intrigue and suspense. She writes for several other publications that inspire about marriage, raising twins, as well as wisdom and life tips. She lives in Birmingham England with her husband and twin sons. For further details and to get help to write your life story or that of someone else, you can contact her by visiting her website at www.writeservice4u.com

OTHER BOOKS BY THE AUTHOR

 **Run For Your Life!** *by Gloria Ekwulugo and Diane Wilkie.* This is the unforgettable story of the ongoing tug of war between good and evil, and Obi's journey from brokeness to destiny. Obi's introduction to life is plagued by poverty and suffering, in the heart of Africa. He therefore becomes obsessed with making it big in life. He naively gets involved in one of the quickest ways to apparently make money and climb to the top. He is introduced to a completely unfamiliar world where he progresses at rocket speed. In an instant his life changes direction, and he is thrust into the terrifying reality that he is in way over his head but it is too late to turn back!

He begins to receive visits from mighty invisible spirit beings that torment and abuse him. Desperate, battered, bruised and just about to walk through death's door, he comes face to face with the most powerful person he has ever met. Is it too late for Obi?

To order your copy please visit:
www.runforyrlife.wordpress.com

Trouble In Paradise *by Gloria Ekwulugo and Diane Wilkie.* This roller coaster ride of romance, adventure and tragedy fill this gripping story from beginning to end. Commencing in the paradise of Jamaica it concludes in the United Kingdom the apparent land of promise Beautiful Cloretta

Cloretta born to a rich family, knows nothing about going without! Leroy, poor and from the wrong social class has nothing to offer her. They fall in love and develop an unrelenting determination to be together against all odds! However their fiery volatile relationship threatens to be a force capable of destroying them both! Cloretta inevitably becomes candle that is dangerously close to being extinguished by the wind that is Leroy. Never did she dream that the price for love might prove to be too high. Passion sweeps her off her feet, and inevitably into a life changing drama of epic proportions! Must Cloretta choose between living her dream or escaping the nightmare?

To order your copy please visit:
www.troublenparadisewordpress.com

ALSO BY OPEN SCROLL PUBLICATIONS

It's Your Time (Your Generatin Awaits You) *by Michael Ekwulugo*

 They say that there's one born every minute. And according to the Bible, each one born, is born a winner. Before your debut on earth, your success had already been settled in heaven. But surviving to succeed at things you were never called to do in this life, is to fail before you've even begun! You've got one life. One opportunity to partner with God and make something spectacular out of your life. There is simply no time to waste.

After reading this book, the next voice the world hears... will be yours!

In this humorous and insightful volume, learn how to:

- Discover, develop and deploy your hidden gifts
- Eliminate the 7 greatest threats to your destiny
- Break free from self-destructive thoughts, patterns and habits
- Manage daunting but essential transitions in your life
- Prepare and position yourself for life-changing opportunities

For more information and to order your copy please visit:

www.ekwministries.co.uk or amazon.co.uk

To Contact the Author

Email: <u>dee.wilkie7@hotmail.co.uk</u>

Visit Blog: nockingonheavensdoor.wordpress.com

If knocking on heaven's door has helped you in any way, please do get in touch as I would love to hear from you.

If you have any prayer requests please make contact, let's pray together!